bless the

broken
road

A STORY OF LOVE, LOSS
AND THE 9/11 TRAGEDY

A MEMOIR

Efthimia McEvoy

ISBN Hardcover: 978-1-7780637-1-8
ISBN Paperback:978-1-7780637-2-5
ISBN Audio:978-1-7780637-4-9
ISBN Ebook:978-1-7780637-5-6

First paperback edition: August 2022

Edited by: Sarah Hutchison
Cover Art by: Rica Cabrex

Printed by: Kindle Direct Publishing

www.blessthebrokenroad.ca

To him, thank you.

Contents

Preface

The best things in life happen when we least expect them. This has been true in my life, thus far. The art is in learning to surrender. Learning to let go of the pressure. Learning that the magic is in how things unfold, and that the outcome can be better than expected when we just let things happen. As cliché as it may be: what is meant to be, will be. And what is meant to leave, will go.

I believe that the concept of coincidence is a comfort to those living on the surface of their thoughts. Everything, whether literally or figuratively, is a sign if you just look deep enough and open up your heart to seeing it. For me, signs often come to me in the form of the number three.

I often feel misunderstood and have never felt as though I fit in. I never felt pretty enough, smart enough, athletic enough or worthy enough. Not only that, I struggled to find love and connection. As I unveil the intimate details of my life, I hope that my painful experiences help others. If sharing my story this vulnerably, helps even one person who is going through heartbreak, it will be worth it.

Chapter 1

"Effie, are you sure you wouldn't rather go to Canada's Wonderland?"

At seven years old, I took a moment to think about that question. I did love going to Canada's Wonderland. Thoughts of seeing the iconic Wonder Mountain, mingling among the Flintstones, going to the Smurf Cave and riding on the teacups were enticing. Yet I had just been to Wonderland and knew it would not compare in the slightest. So, I replied, "Yes, Mom. I want to go to Greece."

I could hear the fear in her voice. The thought of her seven-year-old daughter getting on a plane by herself to go across the world for the entire summer had to be terrifying.

The airport felt big, but not as big as the adventure I was about to embark on. I stood four feet tall with short curly hair and large brown eyes. Before my trip, my mother brought me to the salon for a perm on my short hair. After all, it was the "in" thing to do back in the eighties. I felt like a boy poodle. Even though I had an awful and unfortunate haircut and style, I felt brave and adventurous.

I was yearning to see my favourite cousin, Katerina. She was a couple of years older than me. I looked up to her. She was fun, we laughed a lot together, and she had a great imagination. She taught me how to colour, how to build with Lego, how to design with Lite-Brite, and instilled in me a love for reading. Sometimes, we played well together. Other times, we fought like cats and dogs. She used to live in Canada, rather close to me until her parents decided to move to Greece. We were devastated.

As the plane went up, my stomach went down. With a strong fluttering in the pit of my tummy, I gripped the armrests tightly. My little knuckles were white. I held my breath and squeezed my eyes tight. I didn't dare look out any cabin windows. I could feel the hair on my arms stand tall as the plane engine roared. Once the ascent was complete and my ears stopped popping, I let out a deep sigh. I felt my body begin to relax as I wiggled to get comfortable in the seat. I reached into my tie-dyed backpack and pulled out my favourite book, Corduroy.

It was a long flight, over eleven hours. Because of the distance, my parents paid extra to have a flight attendant take care of me throughout the flight. Their responsibility was to make sure I was given to the correct family upon landing in Athens. I flew with Lufthansa. I had to hand it to them, not only did they get me to my family in Athens safe and sound, but during the flight, they gave me cute paper dolls to play with and lots of extra treats. They made me feel like royalty. They appeared to be at my beck and call, all the while flashing their beautiful pearly white smiles at me and even allowing me to sit with them in the galley on the jump seats. *Wow,* I thought, *I could certainly get used to this!* I was destined to be a jet setter.

Landing in Athens, the journey continued as we made the 40-minute drive from the Athens International Airport to Peristeri, a little neighbourhood tucked amidst the hustle and bustle of Athens, or Athena, as I affectionately knew it. The roads were packed like sardines. The tall buildings, big billboards, the congestion and constant horn honking were like any big city, yet it still fascinated me. My eyes were glued to the window, taking it all in. Part of me was trying to wrap my brain around how I convinced my parents to allow me this incredible opportunity at such a young age. Out of their three kids, I was the oldest and "the most Greek." I embraced the culture and felt proud to have Greek in my blood.

A sense of familiarity rushed through me, telling me we were getting closer to my relatives' home. My heart was beating faster with anticipation, and my smile was ear-to-ear. We arrived at their polykatoikia, a multi-storey apartment building. These were common in Greece, sprawling the streets throughout the entire city. My Theia Angeliki and her husband lived in the top flat. My Theia Chrisoula, her husband, and their two boys Andreas and Mikey lived in the middle. And on the bottom, lived my Theia Stamatoula, her husband, and their three children; Afroditi, Effy and Niko. These were my people. I felt at home.

The architecture was impressive for a city created so quickly with no central planning. Everything seemed to be built the same; with white and grey concrete. There were no elevators; instead, a concrete staircase went from the bottom flat to the top. It reminded me of something out of bedrock.

It could be perceived as cold and lifeless, but within the walls, there was so much love, laughter, happiness and of course the most delicious food.

As I arrived, everyone ran out to the street to greet me. I felt like royalty again. They were excited to see me, but the truth is, I was more excited to see them. Getting reacquainted with my surroundings and family was easy in a way, but also difficult because of the language barrier. I spoke little Greek and they spoke even less English. I understood a little more than I could speak, which led to many awkward interactions. My family in Greece couldn't understand why my father, who was born and bred in Greece, didn't speak Greek to me. Why did he not want his daughter to learn his mother tongue? It was a fair question, and in those awkward moments, I wondered why the heck not either.

I stayed for a week or so in Athena, visiting with my family, being a part of their daily routines. It was enjoyable. I was lucky to spend a lot of quality time with all three of my Theias.

One day, while I was spending time with my Theia Angeliki, she gave me a gold ring with a chocolate opal set in the middle. It was her favourite ring and she wanted me to have it to remember her. I, too, loved this ring. It made me feel special and loved. At this rate, it was going to be difficult to go back to Canada. I was happy to see everyone and grateful to have spent time in Athena, but I couldn't wait to leave the big city and get to the island of Kefalonia! The fresh air, the incredibly delicious food, and the smell of the sea would have anyone excited to get there. I was no exception.

Chapter 2

We were headed out of Athens to catch the ferry that would take us to Kefalonia. Sitting on the bus, I listened to the soft Greek chatter while I enjoyed the beautiful scenery. The trek to get there was long. Eight hours long. However, the scenery and company made it tolerable. The water and the mountains brought a sense of peace and serenity. It was a feeling of calmness that eased any fears or uncertainty I had.

It was a special day, so I wore my favourite outfit. I rocked a pair of hot pink shorts and a white t-shirt adorned with flashy jewels. My thin white socks had a frilly lace trim. My poofy hairstyle completed my look. I was ready to take on the world.

It was a perfect summer day. There wasn't a cloud in the sky. The sun radiated an even heat throughout my body. Underneath the huge boat, the waters were calm. Holding the handrails as I entered the boat, I felt a rush of excitement fill my body. My eyes widened and my smile beamed.

My cousin Mikey and I discovered a bar on the boat that served grilled cheese sandwiches made on a panini press. We thought we had gone to heaven. Many sandwiches later, when our bellies were full, we wandered around the boat as if we owned it, feeling on top of the world. The ferry ride was relaxing. There was something so mesmerizing about watching the front of the boat break through the water. I caught myself staring at the ripple effect of the waves over and over. It was a view I could never get tired of.

Kefalonia is the biggest island in the Ionian Sea, situated west of mainland Greece. The coastline is constructed of limestone cliffs, a winding pattern of bays and strips of beautiful white sand. Its character comes from the incredible sandy coves and dry rough landscapes. The capital of the island is Argostoli, which was built on a hillside overlooking a narrow harbour.

Lixouri however, is where my heart belongs. Located in the northern part of the island thirty-five kilometres west of Argostoli, it is the second-largest village of Kefalonia. The village encircles the blue bay of Argostoli, overlooking the capital. Regular ferries connect the two destinations. When searching for the best spots to enjoy the ocean, Petani Beach is one of its prized possessions because of its spectacular natural beauty. Most beaches on the island are only accessible by foot or by long, narrow twisting roads.

Lixouri is the place that vacationing dreams are made of. It is one of the most picturesque towns on the island, and it offers everything found in a big city - banks, pharmacies, public services and even a hospital. There are also many hotels and studios that cater to all kinds of travellers, preferences and tastes.

This beautiful town receives large numbers of tourists from the beginning of the summer right until the end of the season. An abundance of restaurants and bars, filled with young crowds, line the busy waterfront. The main square - Plateia Petritsi - is the centre of attention surrounded by old-fashioned cafés. Of course, vacationing in Greece means delicious food. In Lixouri, there are many taverns and restaurants that serve delicious traditional Greek cuisine that appeal to even the youngest of customers.

When you venture out of the larger town, you begin to travel through many small villages that add charm and character to the island.

My father grew up in Damoulianata, a small village with less than one-hundred-fifty residents. Its lush nature and high altitude allow for the most stunning sunset views. The panoramic views from the Playia are outstanding. I spent many afternoons watching the sunset and admiring the extraordinary beauty that lay before me. Even at such a young age, I was grateful for this unbelievable opportunity. From our village, it was a quick drive to get to Agia Eleni, a beach five kilometres long with amazing water and a beautiful natural landscape.

After a long day of travel, we finally arrived at the port in Lixouri. We hailed a taxi and off we headed to our little village.

As we were driving along the dirt road, I saw it: A long curved white concrete wall. Immediately I knew my grandparents' home was only seconds away. Right then, I spotted her: Katerina was waiting at the faded burgundy wrought iron gate with the biggest smile on her face. I, too, could barely contain my excitement. I had missed her so much!

I was so grateful to be together with her again. We gave each other a hug that could be felt back in Canada. It was great to see her in the flesh. At the time, I wondered what shenanigans we would get into that summer. Turns out ice cream – a lot of ice cream. There was a quaint convenience store located a few steps from my grandparent's home in the small village. They sold little ice cream cups and there was a hidden toy located in the bottom. Let me just say, that was the cat's meow at seven years old. I felt like in every picture taken that summer, I had an ice cream cup in my hand.

I think that might have been the summer where I developed my sweet tooth. When I wasn't eating ice cream I was introduced to vanilla fondant. It was served on a spoon and called "spoon sweet" or "vanillia". It was dipped in water and licked like a lollipop. It was disgusting, but I still ate it and tried to convince myself it was yummy. After all, it was the social thing to do! There were also these wrapped mini moist chocolate cakes with nuts in them. They seemed to be everywhere. Of course, I indulged. A lot. I guess that's part of the fun of being across the world with no parents. Unlimited treats. Looking back, it makes my stomach hurt.

I quickly learned life in Greece is quite different. Aside from the language, I had the power to go into a convenience store at seven years old to buy cigarettes and alcohol for my older family members. It was shocking to me. My Theia Maria would send Katerina and I daily to buy her a can of Coca-Cola, and every few days a package of cigarettes. Of course, we seized the opportunity to get ourselves ice cream. Looking back, I'm not sure what was worse: the copious amounts of Coca-Cola and cigarettes she consumed or the abundance of ice cream we devoured.

Each afternoon everyone had a siesta! It was an imposed quiet time. Katerina and I had to be quiet in our room usually from twelve to two o'clock. At the time I hated it. It was like punishment without doing anything wrong. As kids, we didn't get it. Now, I get it. What I wouldn't give to have an afternoon siesta every day, to lay in bed and relax without a care in the world.

Imagine not having to think about what to cook for dinner all the while making sure everyone's palate is appeased. Not having to catch up on multiple loads of laundry or making sure the farm animals are well kept and fed. Looking back, I wish I had taken the time to appreciate the 'forced' quiet time.

Katerina and I would often trade our belongings during this time. She would have belongings I loved and I would have belongings she loved, so we would trade! However, most times it didn't end well. We would get upset if the other had our belongings. Eventually, one of us would give whatever it was back and the other wouldn't. Cue the tears.

Sometimes, we would go out into my grandparent's storage shed during siesta time. It wasn't a regular shed; it was special. It felt a lot like a little apothecary, where there were dried wild herbs, preserves, homemade wine and olive oil stored. It was cozy and smelled delicious. We used the shed to play board games in. Katerina taught me how to play Monopoly there. I still remember adamantly saying "no" to purchasing Boardwalk because I thought she was trying to trick me into thinking it was a good property to own. While playing, we enjoyed cracking and eating walnuts from a large burlap bag that I liked to sit beside. It was like our own kid cave. Our happy place.

My Pappou was a very hard worker. He would get up at the crack of dawn every day to head to his farm. He would be planting and sowing seeds of wheat, barley, corn, and other various crops before he tended to the animals. The apple didn't fall far from the tree when it came to hard work. My father was the same as his dad. I marvelled at their ability to do whatever it took to provide for their families.

Pappou's farm was filled with chickens, goats, a cow and my favourite animal, his donkey. He was the sweetest animal. So gentle, patient and loyal. My grandparents didn't have a vehicle, so their donkey was Pappou's means of transportation to and from the farm.

I'll never forget when my Pappou asked if I wanted to have a ride on their donkey. I was few years older than the last time I got to saddle on, and I remember feeling excited but a little nervous. They were large animals. Much larger than I was in my tiny seven-year-old body. However, once I was on the donkey, it felt almost therapeutic in a way. I felt like I was flying. He didn't behave like the typical donkey. He listened intently to my Pappou's direction and kept his pace even slower than normal knowing he was carrying precious cargo. He was gentle and loving. It was hard not to fall in love with such a beautiful animal. I adored him. For the rest of the summer, I enjoyed spending time with him. I learned more and more Greek as the summer went on. I was able to begin to read and was eager to start learning how to write. The Greek language fascinated me. It was so different from what I was used to and I loved the challenge. My Theia Maria played a big role in helping me learn this beautiful language. I was grateful for her willingness and patience to teach me.

When I wasn't learning Greek, hanging out with my cousins, eating ice cream or souvlakia I could be found at the beach. Between all of my aunts and uncles, it seemed like we were at the beach at least three times a week. For good reason! The heat was almost too much to handle. The homes on the island don't have air conditioning, so it was sensible to rely on the coolness of the ocean to keep our bodies from overheating.

One hot summer day, Theia Maria, Katerina and I were sitting at a little table outside on my grandparents' large porch. We were surrounded by beautiful flowers and the overhang from the olive trees. It was the perfect backdrop as I began one of her Greek lessons. It was common in the summertime for homes on the island to leave their front doors open. A curtain was used as a replacement, allowing a breeze into the home. It had been an exceptionally hot summer.

We were right in the middle of my lesson when, all of a sudden, I felt the table jolt. I looked at my Theia with fear in my eyes. I stood up in a panic and flung my arms out as if I needed to keep my balance. I felt the ground beneath my feet shake. The jolt was followed quickly by a shaking that lasted seconds, though it felt much longer. Inside the house, I could hear things tumbling over. I felt paralyzed as I stood on the concrete porch. As quickly as it began, it was over. My little heart was pounding. I had never experienced an earthquake before. Luckily, the damage was minimal. For the rest of the summer, I was terrified another one would strike, possibly causing unimaginable destruction.

Throughout the summer, Theia Maria would take Katerina and me to her friend Christina's home. Christina and her husband Steve had three children, two girls and a boy. Areti was older than us, Rozalia was our age, and Aris was their younger brother. Rozalia, Katerina and I played together the most. I remember many fun times we spent playing. One night, I recall we were having a sleepover at Rozalia's house. We decided it would be fun to start prank-calling people in the villages. It was a lot safer than nicky-nicky-nine doors yet still provided the same thrill. We laughed so hard I thought our guts were going to fall out. Rozalia was always a lot of fun to be around. She had a smile that would light up a room. In her presence, you felt loved, cared for and included.

Every year, August fifteenth was a big celebratory day in Greece, almost as important as Easter. The Panayia is a celebration honoring the Virgin Mary's spiritual sleep and parting from the physical sphere. On this day, churches and chapels, monasteries and nunneries commemorate the passing of the Theotokos or the "God-bearer."

High in the hills in the silent village of Damoulianata is the Playia, where we celebrated this special occasion. The Playia was unique to our village. Once there, you find a family-run restaurant with a balcony that was the home of the most stunning panoramic views of the woodlands and, in the distance, the hazy sea. Also, the Playia in Damoulianata has long been known for the best sunset views on the island. Aside from the restaurant, there is also a wide-open gathering space with a seating area to take in these incredible views.

August fifteenth called for a massive feast, song and dance to celebrate. I looked forward to this day every summer. Greek dancing the Kalamatianos was one of my favourite things to do. The Kalamatianos is one of the most well-known and popular Greek dances. It is performed with all the dancers holding hands in a circle while moving counterclockwise. I felt a great sense of connection to the Greek culture and community.

Our village held one of the biggest celebrations. It was a time when all of my friends, cousins, aunts, uncles and grandparents came together. Katerina, Rozalia and I would have the best time eating delicious souvlakia on sticks, dancing like no one was watching, laughing hysterically and ogling over boys much older than we were. We were footloose and fancy-free.

One thing I didn't like about August fifteenth was that it meant my time on the island was almost over. With school starting in early September, I needed to exit vacation mode and get back into daily routines. Early to bed, early to rise. I needed to adjust to the rules and regulations again, especially after being parent-free for a whole summer.

Consequently, I developed a dislike for goodbyes. It was difficult to leave my friends and family, especially Katerina. I knew we would write letters to each other throughout the year. The excitement of receiving a letter in the mail from her was second to none, however, it just wasn't the same as being able to hug her or eat ice cream while finding something ridiculous to laugh about together.

> *"How lucky I am to have something that makes saying goodbye so hard."*
> - A.A. Milne, from Winnie-the-Pooh

~

Over the next few years, I was fortunate enough to travel to Greece a few more times. Each time, affording me the opportunity of new experiences, quality moments with the people I loved, and an endless supply of the most delicious ice cream and souvlaki on the planet. There was nothing quite like it.

Chapter 3

It was sometime in early May of 1999 when a friend of mine, Gina, asked if I would like to go to Greece with her for the summer. My initial reaction was no. Honestly, we weren't great friends and the thought of going to Greece with her didn't exactly excite me. I felt bad saying no, so I told her I would think about it and let her know.

A few weeks passed and somehow, she convinced me to go. On May 19th our flights were booked. Truth be told, after some time to think about it, I found myself excited.

Gina and I would take trips to local malls to make sure our suitcases were packed full of new attire. I bought a treasure trove of 'going out' clothes. My clothing selection was a little more risqué than hers. I guess one could say the same about our personalities!

She joked a lot about me having a hot summer romance with a tall, dark and handsome Greek man. If there was anything we did agree on, it was our love for such a beautiful country and its men.

The thought of having a hot summer romance was very exciting, but I didn't have any expectations for this vacation. I thought the possibility of it happening to me was pretty slim. Nevertheless, I was grateful I would be able to see my family and friends.

I'm not much of a diary/journal writer, although I wished I was. There are so many benefits to journaling. It is a great form of self-expression that can lift and empower us to understand the intricacies of our feelings. Journaling also helps keep our brain in mint condition. Luckily, as I began on this next adventure to Greece, I faithfully managed to keep a diary for the whole summer.

Dear Diary,

July 6th, 1999
Gina and I made it to Pearson International Airport. My suitcases weighed a tonne. Ready for another adventure, I smiled as I opened the door to the airport. I have zero expectations; therefore, I can't be disappointed. The departure area of the airport had to have been the most depressing, tear-inducing place in there. People were crying as they squeezed their loved ones before having to leave them. I don't know about anyone else, but it made me cry to watch. I could feel their hearts breaking and it made me sad. It was our turn, we said goodbye to my dad, brother and Gina's dad. Even though we would see them at the end of the summer, goodbyes were difficult. As we left them behind and passed through airport security, tears began to stream down our flushed cheeks. Damn it. I didn't want to be that person people felt sorry for. I was fine. I swear it was all the extra emotional energy in the building. I'd done this a time or two before. I was going to make it just fine.

The arrival of our plane was delayed by two hours. We were flying via Olympic Airways, so I couldn't be surprised, since Greeks are notorious for being late.

Sitting in the busy airport in the middle of summer, unsure of what this vacation would hold, I opened my wallet. In it, I carried a picture of my two favourite Ontario Hockey League players Nick Foley and Doug MacIver. It was a reminder of home and the sport I loved so much. In fact, I used to write motivational letters for our local OHL team, the Belleville Bulls. I would sit in my room at my desk until late at night crafting up these letters I thought would be encouraging and then post them on their big metal door before each away game during the playoffs. My goal was to inspire and ignite passion.

My dream of being a sports psychologist stems from the fascination I have for the game of hockey both physically and mentally. I love the speed and skill of the game. The excitement of a breakaway or the back and forth passing of the puck as the final seconds wind down on the clock. There was nothing quite like the energy of the arena when the home team scores. But also, for the goalie who was scored on 6 times, or the team who lost the game. Or when the team was on a losing streak, I want to be the one to fire them up; to turn things around. I want them to be successful, yes, but more importantly, I want them to have a sound mind when the game doesn't end in their favour. Regardless of where it was coming from, there was a lot of pressure on these young athletes. I was ready for the challenge. I knew that coupled with my passion, it would allow me a dynamic, rewarding career path unlike any other.

It was after nine p.m. when we finally started to board the aircraft. The in-flight meal was actually edible: roast beef with pasta, Greek salad and salmon. Not long after dinner, I started feeling nauseous. I pulled out a few Seventeen magazines I made sure to pack into my carry-on bag.

As it turns out, trying to read while feeling nauseous wasn't the best decision. I could feel the colour in my face begin to drain. I glanced over at Gina, her eyes scrunched tight and her nose wrinkled up when she looked back at me. It was a little unsettling. Luckily, I was sitting beside a sweet, older Greek lady. She discreetly handed me a Gravol, tucking it into my hand with a little pat and a smile. I've never taken Gravol, but she's been around the block, I wasn't about to question her. I smiled graciously and mouthed a quiet thank you with a desperate smile on my face. I still had some water left over from my dinner and used it to help me swallow the little pink pill. Despite not being able to sleep, the rest of the flight was smooth sailing.

Chapter 4

July 7, 1999

At last, we had arrived in Athens. We made our way to the luggage carousel, feeling like a bunch of cattle being herded. In true Greek style, we waited an hour for our luggage to arrive. Why did everything have to go at a snail's pace in this country? It was a long flight. Being tired and a little irritated, I looked forward to getting away from the airport.

I spotted my Uncle Bobby. A huge smile donned his face as his thin figure stood there with his arms open wide. Beside him was my cousin Andreas who looked equally as happy to see me. We hailed a taxi and headed to Peristeri. It was five-thirty in the evening when we arrived at my family's home. It had been thirty hours since I had last slept. Up until this point, I hadn't even seen a hot guy. I guess it was better that way since I looked and felt like a zombie. The fact my skin was pale, my eyes sunk in and a rat's nest sat safely on top of my head left no room for anyone to argue.

Being welcomed by my family was such a good feeling. It was so good for my soul. Everyone had grown so much since my last visit. My cousin Afroditi was gorgeous. Her now blond hair lay just past her shoulders, her thin frame and the glow of her makeup-free face had me in awe. Not only was she gorgeous on the outside, but she was even more beautiful on the inside. She was always thinking of others feelings and needs before her own. She made sure you were happy, included and of course fed. One big Greek meal after another. Her heart was made of pure gold, just like her mother. I wanted to be just like her. In my eyes, she was perfect.

Three families lived in one building, so it was easy for us to all be together. It felt so good to be back in their company.

Around midnight, everyone had gone to sleep. Everyone but me, since I was feeling restless and jet-lagged. In an attempt to tire myself out, I turned on the television. I was flicking through the channels, passing Greek show after Greek show. Something caught my attention, so I turned back a channel. The Backstreet Boys were on MTV singing "I Want it That Way" acapella. Another little slice of home that brought comfort and a smile to my face

July 8, 1999

Ten a.m. felt too early to wake up. I hadn't gone to sleep until well after one in the morning. I still felt a little tired. Nonetheless, the adventure must continue. Gina, my cousins and I went to rent a movie. We rented The Game, starring Michael Douglas and Sean Penn. I didn't have the mental capacity to follow along. It was too much for me first thing in the morning in another country. We turned the movie off and decided to play a board game called Hotel. It was a mix between Monopoly and The Game of Life. It was a lot of fun and I won, of course. I was pretty competitive. After that was done, I needed a nap. Once my head hit the pillow, I was out like a light. I slept for several hours.

The aromas of dinner being prepared aroused my senses. My Theia Stamatoula was a skilled cook, much like my father. The food she prepared and served was done with so much love. After dinner, my cousin Effy wanted to take Gina and me to a café. Between taking a bus and lots of walking, it took us nearly an hour to get there. There was a really good-looking guy a few tables away. Throughout the night, I sipped on my delicious, creamy chocolate milkshake, casually glancing over his way. He didn't notice me, but it was nice to finally see some eye candy. We stayed at the café until eleven pm. We had a lot of fun on the jaunt back home. Guys in cars were whistling at us. One guy yelled out the window, "How are my honeys doing?" Not exactly classy, but it stroked our egos and made us giggle.

It was late by the time we arrived home. My cousins Mikey and Andreas bought me a souvlaki in a pita with fries, tzatziki and tomatoes inside. They knew it was my favourite. The chicken was to die for. Spiced to perfection. The smell alone had my mouth watering. I was grateful and my heart and belly were happy.

July 9, 1999

Today I realized the vast majority of vehicles in Greece are ugly. I mean, ugly. Certainly not the same luxury look as what I am used to back home. I am used to seeing big Dodge Ram trucks or large SUVs like my favourite, the Cadillac Escalade. The vehicles here seem so puny and outdated.

July 10, 1999

I woke up to the sound of my cousin Effy calling my name, saying that she wanted to take Gina and me shopping. She told us we needed to take a taxi because it was further away.

We left the house and began to walk down the street. The sun was shining bright. I was wearing a monochromatic blue halter top and a pair of short black dress shorts. I could feel the heat radiating on my arms, neck and legs. We turned a corner and there was a long line of cars parked along the side of the road. Effy was walking ahead of us toward a car. I thought it was a bit strange but followed anyway. She got into the passenger side and motioned for us to get in the back seat. We were puzzled, it didn't look like a taxi but I trusted her so we got in. I looked at the driver and to my surprise, he was a young, handsome Greek guy. Turns out he was Effy's boyfriend. The reason he picked us up there was because if her dad found out she had a boyfriend, he would blow a gasket. She's twenty-two years old. This was blasphemy. I mean, I could sort of understand because my dad is the same way, super strict. I wasn't even allowed to speak to a boy on the phone back when I was in grade ten. However, I would sure hope at the age of 22, I would be allowed to date. They have been dating for the last two years. Her whole family knows, except her father. As unfortunate as this is, it is common in Greece. His name is Adonis and what a gentleman he is. I admired the way he looked at Effy and the way he was so respectful toward her. He was impressive. I am happy they found each other.

We covered every shoe store within an hour radius looking for shoes for Gina. She couldn't find any she liked or that were in her size. We were exhausted and ready for a much-needed break. Adonis took us to a café. Tonight, was the first time in all the years I have been coming to Greece that I felt like an adult.

Located on a busy street, the café was small and comfortable. We laughed and shared stories until it was time to leave. Afroditi was baptizing a baby boy today and we needed to get back to get ready for the special occasion.

Getting ready for the baptism, Afroditi filed and painted my fingernails and toenails. She made me feel like the star of the show. It reminded me of when I was a little girl, when she used to do my hair and give me the prettiest glitter ball hair ties and barrettes to match. I cherished her and our time together.

The baptism went off without a hitch. By the time it was finished, we were famished. Adonis took us out to a pasta house for dinner. I ordered spaghetti and it was delicious. Again, we shared many laughs and great conversation. For the first time, I felt amazing in my skin. Being around these incredible and loving people, I found confidence. I felt sexy and flirty. I felt like I belonged. It was almost two in the morning when we arrived back home. We are leaving for Kefalonia at eight am tomorrow morning. We'll be tired but tonight was by far the best night in Athena.

July 11, 1999
Today is my name day! A name day is a tradition that celebrates the day of the year associated with one's name. The celebration is very similar to a birthday, and in some cases, the Greek people celebrate it more than North Americans celebrate a birthday. An open house is held where a feast is put on for friends and family who come to enjoy it with you. The food and drinks are plenty, followed by dancing.

Seven a.m. was an early start to the day. I was exhausted but looking forward to getting to the island. When we finally arrived in Lixouri, Gina stayed there and I headed to Damoulianta to see my family. I couldn't wait to see them, especially Katerina. I was so close, I could almost feel her energy.

At long last, we were reunited. I could not describe the depth of emotion I felt seeing her. It was the best gift on my name day.

We decided to take a walk to the old school in our village. As we walked along the narrow, now paved road, my eyes stared at the beauty of the stone-built homes covering the length of the walk and how they were finished with red or orange clay tile roofs. Lovely details I hadn't noticed or appreciated when I was younger.

The grounds surrounding the properties were very well kept and traditionally landscaped with whitewashed courtyards garnished with climbing vines and beautiful flower-filled gardens.

We passed the beautiful Church of the Virgin Mary, built in the 1860s. It is an impressive sight in our small village. And we strolled by a few small stores. Thankfully, our quaint little village didn't boast any large hotels, bars or high-rise buildings.

The abandoned playground was just how I remembered it. We sat on the swing set that was kitty corner to the rusted, old merry-go-round. Older now, as a few years had passed since we were last together, we had a lot of catching up to do. We enjoyed great conversation and laughter over a few hours that felt like minutes.

It was getting late when Mikey came to join us. He suggested we go to the Playia to eat souvlakia. He didn't have to twist my arm. I ate three of them. They were so delicious, I wasn't even sorry about it. When in Greece, right?

As the night continued, I was enchanted by the aromas of the evening flowers that filled the streets. Notably, rose and jasmine along with the myriad of aromatic spices like mint and basil. It was comforting and brought me back to the days we were so carefree as we galivanted around the village.

Katerina told me that there is now an internet café in Lixouri. This news was exciting since it meant I would be able to communicate with my friends and family back home. She also said if I wanted to find a guy here on the island, Lixouri was the place to go.

As I looked around, I noticed there were no people in the village, it appeared to be quite boring. I envisioned tumbleweeds blowing down the deserted streets. It looked as though I would be in for a thoroughly monotonous vacation. Yippee.

July 12, 1999

Mikey and I went to Lixouri in the morning. I thought I'd put on my best clothes, just in case I happened to run into my prince charming. Once we arrived into town, we saw Rozalia and Areti. I was surprised and so happy to see them. Immediately I embraced each of them and gave the classic cheek kisses. We didn't have a lot of time to chat but promised to see each other more during the summer. I was looking forward to it.

Mikey and I headed to the internet café. I was excited to compose my first emails from abroad. Shannon, check. Kristi, check. Ashley, check. Doug, check. Emails were sent and I felt quite accomplished. Gina met up with us. She wanted to go shopping. We went into a few stores and then it was time to catch the bus back to the village. Before we left, we made plans for me to come to stay with her and her family in Lixouri tomorrow for five days. I'm hopeful it will be fun.

Tonight, I taught Mikey how to play the Ace to King card game I love. He's a pretty quick learner and makes me laugh a lot. Other than that, I was pretty bored today.

July 13, 1999

I woke up at six-thirty a.m. rushing to get out the door: I had almost forgotten to put on my underwear. I needed to catch the bus to Lixouri. I went to spend five days with Gina but it didn't quite go as planned. She ignored me all day. She and her cousin were whispering and laughing multiple times during the day. Sure, maybe it wasn't about me, but I was excluded. Either way, it was rude. To top it off, she took the film from my camera with pictures I wanted to be developed and 'forgot to ask for doubles'. And, she still wouldn't give me my camera back! Oye vye. Then she and her cousin decided to leave the house to go out somewhere and didn't invite me. Instead, I was left alone with her aunt, whom I didn't know and who couldn't speak English. That was enough for me to pack up my things and go back to my family in my village. I spent the night crying.

I hate it here. I hate waking up here every day. Life is so different here. I just want to go back home. There is nothing here for me. Yes, I love my family here, but I'm ready to go home. I will call tomorrow to see if I can change my flight and get the hell out of here. Peace out.

Chapter 5

July 14, 1999

Today was a day that would change my life forever. I woke up this morning around ten-thirty a.m. I remember not knowing what I was going to do today, other than try to get home.

My sweet Yiayia had made breakfast for me, then I decided to bring my book outside to read for a while. I enjoyed reading and being able to do so in peace. My Yiayia and Pappou kept a bed out on their porch. It was perfect for taking afternoon naps or relaxing while reading. My Yiayia loved to sit outside on the bed and crochet blankets. You could feel the breeze through your hair and smell the salt of the ocean in the air. A large olive tree provided the perfect amount of shade over the bed to shield the hot sun. My best friend from back home, Shannon, had given me a Chicken Soup for the Soul to read while I vacationed. I didn't get far into the book before my cousin Mikey came along and asked if I would play cards with him. We played for a bit, then went to Katerina's house where we also played Pictionary, as well as many more card games.

It was a stiflingly hot afternoon so, naturally, Katerina, Mikey and I decided to go to the beach. It was only my third day on the island and I hadn't been to the ocean since my last visit a few years ago, so I was excited to go back. It was the perfect place to take my mind off of wanting to go back home to Canada.

We went to the local beach of our village, Agia Eleni. It is a smaller beach that the locals visit. The road to get there was super narrow and windy. My uncle has a little white truck, similar to a Chevy S10. We piled in the back and hung on for dear life. We ducked and swerved to avoid the olive trees, and we sang and laughed at the top of our lungs. It was so liberating. We felt like we were on top of the world.

When we made it to the beach, I felt a flood of excitement. I took in the pristine, unadvertised beauty before me – the red rock cliffs and the white pebble beach. I couldn't wait to be blessed by the salt waters of this ocean I had missed so much.

If you're brave enough to walk through a jungle of huge slippery rocks, there is a little secluded area. Of course, we ventured to that part of the beach. Katerina and I were alone lying on the sand, chatting, laughing and making plans for our summer together. She was trying her best to convince me to stay.

At one point, I remember getting up and going into the water. Feeling the saltwater crash against my body was refreshing. The emerald and turquoise colours had an instant calming effect on me. It had been far too long since I felt the magic of the ocean in and on my body. I stood against a large rock in my lilac-coloured bikini. I had traded in my boy poodle look for long, flowy dark hair. I felt beautiful; sexy even.

I felt a sense of freedom. Just me and the depths of the salty waters welcoming me like an old friend. Then, out of nowhere, this Greek god came from the water around the large rock and stood directly across from me. We made eye contact and I felt my stomach hit my toes. He began walking toward me. I felt paralyzed. Unable to move, unable to breathe or think. He was drop-dead gorgeous. He was like something out of a dream. He looked at me and in Greek asked me if I knew what time it was. The way he smiled and looked at me was like nothing I had ever experienced. It felt like pure magic. My mind couldn't register what he was saying quickly enough, as I was so taken aback by his beauty. I had forgotten all of the Greek I knew. There was a pause and then he asked me in English. I remember giggling, feeling like a complete idiot. I finally responded to him in Greek in my sweetest, most nervous voice, that it was six pm. He laughed, said thank you, and waved goodbye with a wink. And with that, he was gone back into the water like some sort of godly magical sea creature. My heart was pounding. A smile from ear to ear was frozen upon my face. It took me a few minutes to comprehend what had happened. I needed to pull myself together. However, I knew the buzzing I felt in my body wasn't going anywhere any time soon.

It was time for us to go back up to the village to help prepare for dinner. I remember standing in the back of the truck bed on the way up the mountain as we left the beach. I said to Katerina, I am going to marry him. She rolled her eyes and laughed at me. She reminded me that I didn't even know his name. I had no idea how I was ever going to see him again, but I knew for certain, in my heart, I would. Our eyes may have met, but our souls instantly connected.

July 15, 1999

I was extremely tired this morning. I didn't sleep a wink. I could not stop fantasizing about him – the Greek god and our magical meeting, that happened seemingly out of nowhere. I had made plans with Katerina to go to Lixouri early in the morning. I soon regretted it when she came to get me at six forty-five a.m.

The bus arrived in our village at seven a.m. I was positive I would be running on adrenaline all day.

To think I wanted to be on the next flight out of here less than twenty-four hours ago is wild. I'm so glad I wasn't. The universe has something better in store for me. Patience is a virtue.

It was great to spend the day out shopping with Katerina. We always laughed so much when we were together. Before heading back on the bus to the village, I made a stop at the internet café. I finally received an email from Shannon. Technology is pretty amazing. I loved being able to keep in touch with her while being across the world.

When I got back to my Grandparent's home, Yiayia had made my absolute favourite Greek meal: Pastichio. It's a layered baked dish that includes a medley of spices in a tomato sauce, with penne pasta noodles, ground beef and bechamel sauce. It was as delicious as it was comforting. My stomach was so full, yet I couldn't resist another piece of this yummy masterpiece.

Later that night, Katerina and I were getting ready to go to meet up with some friends. I cherished being around all the girls. It felt like a sisterhood. We enjoyed sitting around at the Playia talking, laughing and being together.

It was around ten-thirty p.m. when, all of a sudden, we heard motorcycles coming through the village. Through the darkness, the shine of big headlights came straight toward us.

They stopped within a few feet of us. We all looked at each other like, who the heck are these guys rolling into the village so late at night? One took his helmet off and ran his hand through his hair. Low and behold there he was, the godly man from the beach. What?! I was witnessing a magical divine orchestration right before my freakin' eyes. I instantly felt the heat in my body rise from the tips of my toes to the top of my head. My heart was pounding, my hands were sweaty, and I remember I wasn't able to do or say anything but smile. My eyes felt as big as the ocean. I remember feeling so incredibly happy but wondered how the hell it was happening. How did he know where to find me, and so quickly? How did he know? I couldn't believe my eyes! Was I dreaming?

He was absolutely, unequivocally beautiful. Hands down, the sexiest man alive. Period. His body, his smile and those eyes of his melted my heart immediately, again. Unfortunately, he and his friend didn't stay long and I didn't pull it together fast enough to get his name. The girls were giddy for me! Gushing, they told me they felt the spark between us. I couldn't disagree, and based on the smile he gave me and the look in his eyes, I could confidently say it wouldn't be my last opportunity to find out his name.

I couldn't sleep. He captivated me. But who was he? I had never met someone who made me feel this way. He was so handsome, so seemingly perfect. I lay in bed staring at the ceiling unable to stop smiling. My lucky number was three, and what do you know, three days on the island and I meet my dream man? Coincidence? I don't think so. This was my sign from the universe. Unlike summers past, I was sure copious amounts of ice cream was not what I would be indulging in this summer.

Chapter 6

July 16, 1999

I found myself lying in bed for most of today with a smile stuck on my face. I wondered if I would be graced with his presence tonight? I surely hoped so.

The phone rang, and it knocked me back into reality. It was Katerina! She asked if I wanted to go to Space with a group of our friends. I laughed and told her that is kind of where I felt like I had been all day! Space is a popular dance nightclub on the island.

That afternoon there was a distinctive aroma that filled my grandmother's home. My taste buds were watering and I knew exactly what it was. Yiayia made another one of my favourite Greek dishes, Yemista. It's stuffed tomatoes. Each tomato was stuffed with ground beef, rice, onions, garlic and a blend of spices and baked in a pan with roasted potatoes. They are juicy, healthy, and bursting with fresh colours and flavours. Is it any wonder my father owns a successful restaurant in Canada? He has learned from the best!

I started getting ready to go out for the night. I was excited to go dancing. Thanks to my strict father, I had never been to a nightclub before, much less one on an island in Greece. I was kind of nervous.

It took some effort to pull myself together as my grandparents' home was an older building from the ancient civilization of Greece. It was not equipped with many of the modern luxuries of houses today. For instance, before taking a shower, I needed to turn on the water heater and wait thirty minutes for the water to heat up. Then I needed to get a bucket from outside to stand in under a pipe that would spit out the water for my shower. When I wanted to shave my legs, I filled a bucket of water outside and stretched my leg up onto the concrete wall of the house. My grandparents didn't have any neighbours in their backyard or beside them who would have caught a glimpse of what I must have looked like. Although, I'm pretty liberal and honestly it wouldn't have bothered me at all. I took pride in taking care of myself. I'm learning it's important for me to feel good in my skin and body. So, if that meant doing some acrobatic work outside in the heat of summer while shaving my legs, so be it. Also, there is no flushing any toilet paper down the toilet. Instead, it gets put into a garbage bin beside the toilet. This was simply because their sewage pipes are half the size of Canadian plumbing. I had to hand wash my clothes in a bucket outside. One bucket with detergent and a washboard and the other bucket with clean water for rinsing. Hang to dry.

When I think about how privileged I am to experience life growing up in Canada in the twentieth century with modern technology, I realize I simply take for granted items such as a washing machine, dishwasher, fancy rain head shower and even being able to flush toilet paper down the toilet. I feel incredibly blessed. Not only to have these luxuries back home, but to also have the opportunity to realize how fortunate I am. Life wasn't easy for my Grandparents or for most people of their generation and the generations that came before them. I could deal with having to put a little muscle behind these necessary tasks. I could even get used to not being able to flush the toilet paper down the toilet. There have been far too many people before me who have suffered and worked ridiculously hard with much less. It was the least I could do. I was blessed.

I kissed my grandparents goodbye and skipped to Katerina's house. Once she was ready, all dolled up, we left the village and headed to Lixouri. The cafés lined the large square. Hundreds of tables were perfectly placed setting the scene and atmosphere for a great night. We found a café that had room for all of us and promptly ordered some drinks. I ordered a vodka orange. It was a chill vibe as we laughed and spent time with great people. Now, I felt like I was living the life. It was after midnight when we headed to the club. Surprisingly, when we arrived not many people were there yet. Not to worry; by one-thirty a.m. the club was full.

I was having fun, enjoying being in the company of my friends, but in the back of my mind, I couldn't stop thinking about him. Did he go to my village looking for me? Would he come back tomorrow night? Would I ever see him again? The thought of not seeing him ever again made me feel sick to my stomach. There was something about him. The magnetic force I felt when he was around was off the charts. There was no denying it. I remained confident he would be back, our connection felt too strong for that to be it.

July 17th, 1999
Another day had passed and I didn't see him.

July 18th, 1999

Mikey and I played many card games. He was such a sweet little guy! I have the best cousins! Nevertheless, I had enough cards for one day. I got my book and went to the Playia alone. I found such comfort in reading a good book. It helped to occupy my mind as I waited for night to fall. The sunsets in our village at the Playia truly are spectacular. As the sun was going down, it became more and more difficult to read. I found my eyes gazing into the horizon, taking in the beauty. How incredibly lucky was I in those moments?

It was getting a bit chilly so I went to Yiayia's house to pick out a sweater and headed to get Katerina. Turns out she didn't feel like going out. I put my persuasive pants on and finally, after forty-five minutes, I convinced her to come up to the Playia with me.

As we walked up the staircase leading to the Playia, we noticed a lot of people were there! It was normally much quieter. We saw our friends hanging out, but then I spotted two motorcycles and my stomach dropped. I began acting erratically. My arms and legs felt like Jello. I was excited, nervous and over the moon with happiness. Katerina looked at me as if I were a lunatic. I couldn't help it. My hormones were in overdrive and I was about to be in the presence of a Greek god to whom I felt this wild connection.

As soon as I sat down our eyes locked, and with a big smile on his face, he said, "Awe, you're the one from the beach," complete with a wink I'm not sure could get any sexier. Not to mention his accent! My heart was pounding. I felt tingling all over my body. My friend Julia whispered "relax" in my ear.

I tried to relax. I tried really hard. It was no secret at this point – it was loud and clear how I felt about him. I could honestly say I had never, ever felt this way about another human being in my entire life. It was an enchanting feeling.

Julia was excited watching this all unfold. She, too, had a huge smile on her face. She did the honours of introducing us. I was so glad she broke the proverbial ice. His name is Alexandros. He lives in the village right beside mine. What are the chances? He and his family come to their home on the Island for the summer. He has a summer job working at Daphne's restaurant at the best beach on the island, Petani. When the summer is over, he and his family go back to their home in Athens where he attends school. I couldn't wait to learn more about him, I wanted to know everything. Alas, I would need to wait at least another day. After almost an hour, it was getting late. He and his friend needed to go. He looked me right in the eyes and said, "Goodnight." I could have died.

July 19th, 1999

I woke up at six a.m. this morning. Katerina and I were headed to Argostoli. She had errands she needed to run and I wasn't prepared to miss spending time with her. When we got to Lixouri I had my regular jambon and tiri (ham and cheese) sandwich. It's like the world-famous spanakopita but with ham instead of spinach. It was delicious.

We caught the ferry over to Argostoli at eight a.m. Katerina and I were chatting on the boat, and I could sense she was a bit off. Then, with tears in her eyes, she confided in me that she hated her life in Greece. She wanted so badly to move back to Canada. I felt bad for her. I tried my best to console her and let her know should she ever come to Canada, she would be welcomed with open arms. It was a bit selfish on my part. I wanted her to move back to Canada as much as she did. Although being on the ferry staring at the gorgeous scenery before me, it seemed odd that one would hate living here so much. I was, however, wearing my rose-coloured glasses.

We weren't back in our village long before Katerina's brother called to see if I wanted to go to the beach. He said they were going to go to Petani. Did I ever! I couldn't pass up the opportunity to see Alex. The car was full of our friends, laughter and great music. I may or may not have been emitting some nervous and excited vibes as we headed to the beach.

I saw him, working in his element. His smile could be seen from miles away. He looked so happy, so full of life. His energy was contagious. As I lay out on the beach, I couldn't take it anymore. I needed to go up to the restaurant to see him. I decided I would go and grab a drink for a friend and I. I wanted something with vodka in it, but they only had beer. I don't drink beer, but beer it was. I ordered two Heineken and then left him a tip. I tried hard to play it cool but may not have pulled it off, especially when I went back to the beach and stared at him for the next few hours. We left the beach around four p.m., and sadly that was the last time I saw him for today.

July 20th, 1999

I slept until one p.m. today. I woke up to the sound of the phone ringing. It was my cousin asking if I wanted to go to the beach again! How lucky am I? Of course, I did! And, I'm sure by the squeal in my voice, he understood my excitement.

Alex was hard at work again today. It was a busy restaurant. I enjoyed watching him laugh, smile, and move his hips swiftly around the tables, as he delivered food and checked for satisfaction.

Sitting under the hot Grecian sun in the middle of the afternoon left us parched. I went up to the restaurant to pick up a couple of peach iced teas for Katerina and I. I couldn't possibly pretend to like beer again. I tried hard to be cute, but I'm sure I came across as a little crazy. He must like crazy because he wouldn't let me pay for the peach iced teas. I was surprised, and definitely flattered. Was this another sign he was into me? I felt nervous around him, in a good way though. My insides were singing and doing the biggest happy dance. When I am around him, something feels so right.

We stayed at the beach for hours. I played ball and frisbee in between watching him work. I was in complete awe.

Alex left the restaurant and came down the path that led to the rocky beach. I could see he was headed to the water for a swim. His body. OH my, his body. I imagined what an incredible lover he would make. He oozed sexiness. I'm not sure if I will ever be lucky enough to find out. Thoughts of him and I together began racing through my mind. I wanted so badly to touch him, to feel his body against mine. I was a raging ball of hormones.

That night, Katerina and I walked up the long staircase to the Playia. About halfway up, I could smell the lemon, garlic and oregano seasoning of the souvlakia cooking on the outdoor grill. It was an irresistible waft. My mouth was watering. We met up with all of our friends in our usual spot. We couldn't resist the delicious smell and all decided to eat souvlakia together. I was secretly awaiting his arrival. Okay, maybe it wasn't a secret. It was after one a.m. and there were no signs of him. Was I too much for him? Did I scare him? Did he have a girlfriend? So many thoughts and insecurities ran through my mind. At that moment, I decided I couldn't let these negative thoughts overtake my mind. I needed to remain positive and confident. With that realization, I said goodnight to the girls and headed home. My pillow was calling.

Chapter 7

July 21st, 1999

Today, my day began at the internet café in Lixouri. I wanted to send an email to Shannon to keep her up to date on the Greek god I had found here. The clickety-clack of my fast fingers on the keyboard echoed throughout the café. I was fired up and there was so much I needed to fill her in on. I also registered myself for ICQ and hoped my contacts would be there when I signed in. Having the opportunity to chat with my friends in real-time would be great. My fingers were crossed.

Katerina, Kosta and I went to the beach again this afternoon. Although we didn't go to Petani, we went to our village beach, Agia Eleni. I was disappointed, though it was nice to be at the beach with all of our friends. There were twelve of us hanging out, playing ball, laughing and having a great time together. We didn't leave the beach until six-thirty p.m. I was exhausted by the time we got home. I didn't want to do anything. Then thoughts of missing Alex at the Playia motivated me to get my act together. I got ready and headed to Katerina's house. She, of course, wasn't ready, but to be fair, she didn't quite have the same motivation as I did. While she was getting ready, we had the funniest conversation of my life. I'm not sure I had ever laughed so much. Ever. I was able to be so real and honest with her. Consequently, we were able to have the best conversations. I could trust her and I knew she felt the same. We understood one another.

Around nine-forty-five p.m., I suggested we go up to the Playia to get souvlakia, because I was hungry. My whole being also hungered to see a certain someone!

My timing was impeccable. With our souvlakia in hand, we walked down the stairs of the restaurant to the Playia. My eyes saw two motorcycles that weren't there when we went up. It's incredible how quickly excitement can escalate in my body. My main concern was: How would I ever eat this souvlaki in front of him?

Our eyes locked and he said, "Hi, how are you?" I'm sure I managed to sputter out something in response. He then said he was cold. Cold? My body felt like it was a hundred-fifty degrees. I'd surely warm him up. But I recognized we weren't there. Yet.

He and his friend went up to get souvlakia and I took the opportunity to eat mine as quickly as I could. My friends got a kick out of watching me shovel the souvlaki in my mouth so fast. I inhaled it. Not sure there was even much chewing happening.

When he and his friend got their souvlakia, they left on their motorcycles. What the hell? What a tease. I imagined he was having the same anxieties about eating in front of me, as I had about eating in front of him. They were not gone for long. They were back within ten minutes. Watching him drive his navy-blue Honda motorcycle got me excited. I could feel a rush to my nether region and immediately felt pulsing begin. It felt good. So. Damn. Good. He was incredibly sexy. I mean really, I didn't think he could get any sexier. Turns out I was wrong. He kept bringing the sexy and I was not complaining.

When they came back to the Playia, they parked a little bit away from us. I think they were hoping we would come over to them. We didn't. We were waiting for them to come to us. They didn't. So they left. I was upset they left, but also that I was too shy to go over to him.

July 22nd, 1999

Waking up this morning, I was so sore. Every bone in my body was aching and I was hungry in so many ways. Yet only one was in my control - food.

I inhaled a cold stuffed tomato and some roasted potatoes. It seemed like a good idea at the time, but I quickly regretted my breakfast decision as it hit my stomach.

I got dressed and headed to see Katerina. We played a lot of card games. We probably played for five hours straight. I had enough. My brain was fatigued. I puttered around the rest of the day with my cousins, enjoying the time I was spending with them. Around seven-thirty p.m. I started to get ready for the night. Katerina and I concluded that Alex would come to our village tonight.

The two of us made our way to the Playia to our usual hangout spot. There were eight of us girls. Our sisterhood. The laughs flowed freely and love was felt abundantly. At ten p.m, dare I say I wanted to go get souvlakia? Every freakin' time I go to get a souvlaki, he shows up. I saw him and immediately became unhinged. He looked into my eyes and said, "How are you?" I am not sure if my response was coherent. I felt lost in his eyes. They were twinkling in the light of the dark sky. He and his friend stayed for about half an hour and I didn't speak.

I wanted to. I so badly wanted words to come out of my mouth. I was nervous. All I could do was stare at his beauty. I felt as though he was as shy as I was. Through all of this, I felt there was something magical happening between us.

Watching him drive away on his motorcycle brought a dreary feeling to my body. Each time it got more and more difficult to see him go. It was only Katerina and I left at the Playia. As much as I loved our group, I quite enjoyed our quiet time together. When we could be our true, raw selves with one another. Katerina was a lot more introverted than I was, so I appreciated everything she was able to share with me during these times.

I thought about how romantic it would be to have a boyfriend here. There are so many fun, secluded places to go. I have this insane fantasy Alex and I are going to get together. He picks me up on his motorcycle and we drive to the most beautiful, romantic place on the island. We would be holding hands, sharing our goals, dreams and desires. Kissing and touching one another mixed between glances at the beautiful night sky. Then he'd bring me home, passionately kiss me goodnight and tell me he would pick me up the next day for another adventure together. My ultimate goal is to make love to him on the beach at night. I feel as though that would never happen, but if it did, it would be a dream come true.

July 24th, 1999
This morning my Pappou woke me up at 6:15 a.m. because I had let him know yesterday that I wanted to take the seven a.m. bus into Lixouri. With only three and a half hours of sleep, I dragged myself out of bed. I looked in the mirror and thought I might look better if I were hit by a Mack truck. I pulled myself

together enough to make it to Lixouri. There were errands I needed to get done.

My cousin Mikey accompanied me and drove me batty. He was cute but also knew how to get on my nerves. He was like my little brother. We were in Lixouri for five hours together with nothing to do but wait for the stores to open up. It was very poor planning on my part.

While at the internet café, I was able to send out four emails quite coherently given my sleep deprivation. I was proud. I needed to pick up a roll of film I had developed, which cost a whopping fifteen dollars. Lastly, I needed to stop by a pharmacy to pick up some skincare. I felt as though my face needed all the help it could get at this point.

Finally, we arrived back at the village. I walked as quickly as I could to the house, sweltering in the heat. I flopped on the bed and let out the biggest sigh.

I wasn't on the bed for five minutes when Katerina called and said we were going to Petani to swim. I looked and felt like a hot mess. However, I quickly gained my second wind. With a pep in my step, I was fired up! Let's go!

While we were out in the morning, I bought a beach racquet set. I was going to get a chance to show off my skills on the beach in front of everyone! What could go wrong?

We arrived and I immediately saw him. It was tough taking my eyes off of him. Of course, whenever anyone wanted anything, I voluntarily went up to the restaurant to order. In between my trips to the restaurant, I played frisbee, tennis, ball and I swam. We made small talk and then he asked me if I was going to Space that evening. I blurted out, yes, without having any idea if I was or how I would get there. Luckily, later, when I asked my cousin Kosta, he said they had planned to go. The stars kept aligning.

We left the beach at five-thirty p.m. As soon as I arrived home, I started getting ready to go out. Thoughts raced through my mind of how the night would go. I imagined dancing with him, being close enough to touch and smell him more intimately. My body was full of excitement thinking about it. I had to look my best. I wanted him so badly. The chemistry and sexual tension was too much to handle for any length longer. I needed a release and I was hoping he felt the same.

At eight-thirty p.m, Kosta, Katerina and I, along with Eleni and Christina, left the village and headed to Lixouri. We would stay in Lixouri at a café until around one a.m. and then we made our way to Space. I worried we were going to miss him since it was so late, however, everyone assured me this would not be the case.

When we arrived, the club was empty. The music was blaring, the vibe was great and I, well, I had a huge pit in my stomach. All of a sudden, I became incredibly nervous. I didn't know what to expect. I found a seat facing the door so I could keep my eyes peeled for his arrival.

Low and behold, there he was. He entered the club but he wasn't alone. Who was she? He wouldn't possibly ask me if I was going to the club and then bring his girlfriend? Would he? Was this his way of saying he wasn't interested? That the chemistry I had been feeling wasn't being reciprocated? I thought I might vomit. I wanted to crawl into a hole and die. I needed to take a second to pull myself together and just trust.

As I continued to watch the situation unfold, I noticed he wasn't touching her and they weren't even dancing close to one another. Was it a new relationship? I had no idea what to make of what I was watching. Just trust, I thought to myself.

Why did he have to look so damn sexy? I couldn't take my googly eyes off of him. I was terrible at being inconspicuous. I wasn't expecting a call from the CIA asking to be their newest recruit, that's for sure.

My friend Julia came over to me because she was trying to set me up with another friend of ours who was from our village. Apparently, he liked me a lot but didn't want to say anything because I was always being so vocal about my feelings for Alex. I politely declined. If there was anyone I was going to have a hot summer romance with, it was going to be with Alex. She seemed disappointed, but I wasn't about to settle. My heart was set.

The girl he was with had left, and I noticed he was looking around. I had turned my back for a second, and when I turned back around, he was walking toward me. I must have looked like a deer caught in headlights. He came up to me and asked if I wanted to come dance. Then, looking me dead in the eyes, he asked why I didn't go dancing with him earlier as he smiled at me. My heart dropped. He knew I was staring at him and wondered why I wasn't shooting my shot. Excellent. However, this also meant the girl he arrived at the club with wasn't a love interest of his. Phew.

We made our way to the dance floor. I was extremely nervous. Truthfully, I was a horrible dancer. I didn't have a lot of experience. Growing up, my dad was strict. I was never allowed to even speak to boys on the phone, much less go to school dances or anything of the sort. So, to be in this environment, in the hottest club on the island in front of this godly man, had me in a ball of nerves.

As soon as we got on the dance floor, he took my hands into his. Our bodies moved closer simultaneously. Our hands intertwined, and we moved together with the music. I could feel the nervous sweat dripping down my body. Maybe it was all in my head? I don't know. All I know is that I felt like I was going to collapse. We were looking right into each other's eyes; but it was more than that. We were looking into each other's souls, as we had many times before. I felt as though I was in an alternate universe. I thought I was going to fall to the floor into a big puddle. His eyes were the most gorgeous eyes I had ever seen. His hands were incredibly soft, it was as if I was holding human silk. He kept telling me I was doing great.

We were two perfect strangers, and in that moment the world stood still. There are no words to describe how he made me feel or how comfortable I was. I didn't want it to end. I told him I never dreamed I would be here with him, to which he responded that it was his honour. Ah, be still my heart. He was my knight in shining armour. He was simply perfect.

The music switched back and forth between English and Greek. I had lost track of time until Kosta came and told me it was time to go. Alex saw Kosta come up to me and then asked if I was leaving. I responded with a sad head nod, yes. He took my hands into his and we got lost in each other's eyes. It was as if we were the only two in the club. I have never felt a stronger connection or a higher sexual tension in my entire life. He said he would see me tomorrow. My body was vibrating. I was craving him, every single part of him.

Tonight I had a taste of something so electric, so real – something that breathed life back into me.

Chapter 8

July 25th, 1999

He was my last thought before I went to sleep and my first thought when I woke this morning. It was safe to say, I was smitten. Today couldn't possibly go by fast enough. I wanted it to be nighttime now.

My cousins took me to a new beach today. Xi. It's a dark red sand beach, which I loved. It was a nice change from the rockiness of both Petani and Agia Eleni. However, it was missing one important element, Alex.

Katerina and I were hit on by a few older men, who were relentless. It wasn't a good look for them. She knew one of them and allegedly they were quite well to do. I was definitely not interested. Not even a little bit.

Lying there on the soft sand, listening to the waves crash, brought me right to my fantasy with Alex. An intense flood of goosebumps overtook my body. There was something about the water that made everything much more magical.

My body was covered in sand. I needed to take a shower. After I washed, I did my hair and makeup in great anticipation of my meet-up with Alex. Feeling ready for the night, I went to get Katerina.

Alex arrived at my village with a friend and I gathered the courage to go over to him alone. We both had giant smiles on our faces. He had come right from working a twelve-hour shift to see me. I was both impressed and honoured. As we looked deep into one another's eyes, I wanted to tell him so badly how I felt about him and how incredible I felt around him. My friends advised me not to do so and as hard as it was for me to hold back my feelings, I took their advice. We had the chance to chat, get to know one another and we did a lot of eye gazing. I could stare into his eyes forever. His body was simply the most beautiful work of art. I wanted to touch, feel and explore every single inch of him.

Although nothing groundbreaking happened between us tonight, I was grateful for the time we got to spend together. Every time we see each other, it gets better and better. I was a virgin, but his eyes, smile and the way he carried himself brought out my inner sex kitten.

July 27th, 1999
Since I didn't see Alex yesterday, I knew today I would see him. I didn't wake up until twelve-thirty in the afternoon. Granted, I didn't get to bed and fall asleep until the wee hours of the morning.

My Yiayia was out on the front porch crocheting a blanket. She and my Theia Maria both loved to crochet. They created beautiful work. I often wished I knew how or took the time to learn. I had a quick conversation with my Yiayia before I headed to Thea Maria's. She had made a turkey dinner that smelled delicious. We all sat around the table to eat this wonderful feast. It seemed weird in the middle of summer to be eating a turkey dinner! However, I wasn't going to complain, it was delicious.

After we finished eating, Katerina let me know we were going swimming at Petani. I was super thrilled. I couldn't clean up the dishes fast enough!

The drive to get there was beautiful, going through little villages along the way. The roads were so narrow at times you thought you were going to fall down the mountain. I prayed a lot that we didn't come across another car coming in the opposite direction. I didn't want to die. Not today.

Ah, at last, there he was. He was beautiful. Everything about him shined. He radiated such incredible energy and charm. Our eyes met and he smiled and waved. I was in Heaven. My heart was beating fast. Katerina, Kosta, Irini, Christina and I headed down the path to the water. The waves were big. Humongous actually. Despite the waves being at least 8 ft tall, I made a senseless decision to go sit in the water. Immediately I was pulled in and thrown around by the force. To say I was scared shitless was an understatement. As another huge wave came barreling over me, my bikini top was whipped off. I then felt my head bounce off of a large rock in the water. It felt like I was a little sock in a giant washing machine. I actually thought I was going to die. I didn't know how or when I was going to get my next breath. Kosta ran in to save me and all I could think of was I hoped Alex wasn't watching this embarrassing scene unfold. Thankfully I made it out alive, but that did it for me, I wasn't going to brave the sea again. Ever. Well, at least not when the waves are eight feet tall.

After such a traumatic incident and a few games of ping pong on the beach, Irini was hungry so we went up to the restaurant. Alex came over to take our order. Gosh, he was adorable. I was one smitten kitten. The way he looked at me got my heart pumping.

The restaurant was busy yet he made us feel like we were the only ones there. We didn't order a lot. Two plates of fries and two drinks. I would have easily ordered a giant spread if it meant I would be able to stay in the restaurant longer. Nonetheless, Irini wanted to grab and go. Before we headed back to the water, I asked him if he was going to come to my village tonight, to which he replied yes, he was going to come as soon as he was finished working. Oh gosh, I feel like this beautiful slow build is turning into something pretty great.

Looking in the mirror as I was getting ready for his arrival, it was impossible to get the smile off my face. I didn't know if I had ever been this happy in my entire life. Lastly, I put on my L'Oreal lash out mascara to complete my look and gave myself one last smile in the mirror before bolting out the door.

I could not wait to see him. I felt like tonight was going to be different. I felt like the magnetism between us was going to pull us in even closer. There is nothing I wanted more than to feel his lips upon mine. I hoped I was right.

As I was at the Playia waiting, Julia and Alexandra showed up. I let them know Alex had told me he was going to come tonight to see me. They were surprised and very happy for me. Julia created a plan. If Alex came alone, they were going to leave us so that we could have time together. I thought it was a great plan.

I heard one motorcycle come through the village. My heart began to race. I couldn't contain the wildness I felt inside of my body. Calm, I thought to myself. Now is not the time to bring the crazy out.

He showed up with another girl. My heart sank. However, he wasn't long in introducing us to his cousin Cassie.

She was beautiful. Her smile was beaming and her presence was welcoming. I wasn't sure why she was there. How would we get time alone? I couldn't imagine she would want to be a third wheel.

As we sat around chatting with one another, Julia suggested we all go to the old school. I liked the idea. It was a bit of a walk and maybe I'd get the chance to chat with him on the way. Although I wished it were only the two of us walking through the moonlit village at ten o'clock at night, the camaraderie was fulfilling.

As we continued to walk, Alex asked everyone to walk ahead of us. It was like he could read my mind. Once we arrived at the school Alex and I sat on a bench together. Looking into his eyes was my favourite view. Neither one of us could stop smiling. He asked me if I wanted to go for a walk. Would I ever, I thought. Blushing, I replied with a definite yes.

We left the school and as we carried forward with our walk, he said it. The words I could not wait to hear. The words would send shocks up and down my body. I like you. Finally! Looking into his beautiful eyes, feeling my heart beating out of my chest, I expressed to him I liked him as well. He continued by saying he had liked me since the first time he saw me back at the ocean when he asked me what time it was. Yes! I thought to myself. I knew I felt the enormous spark between us. Getting that confirmation from him felt so gratifying. It's been a slow burn, a beautiful build-up. But to finally hear the words come out of his mouth and to be able to tell him I was feeling the same was so damn fantastic. He also said everyone knew he liked me but he was too shy to say anything.

We continued to walk to the next village, where there was another abandoned school. We were all alone and took a seat on a bench in the playground. We sat facing one another. Our arms were around each other, our bodies so close and my head was resting on his broad shoulder. My hand began massaging his back. I could feel his heart beating and I'm sure he could feel mine. He said it's a full moon tonight. I couldn't say anything at all. I was so speechless as his hand was playing with my hair and caressing my face and shoulder. It felt so incredibly right being with him. A little surreal.

Looking into my eyes like only he could, he said, I want to kiss you. Still speechless, I closed my eyes and felt my trembling lips touch his. It was happening, we were kissing. The warmth of his mouth radiated through me. It felt as though our lips were taking a slow, sensual passionate walk through the park. Only stopping to capture glimpses of the beautiful scenery along the way. The release of this pent-up desire I had for him felt like the moment a volcano erupts. Every part of me was tingling and I could feel the pounding of my heart and wondered if he felt it too. I was hot and moist in all the right places, and I desperately wanted him to feel that.

After the kiss, we sat there in a silent embrace and then he kissed my forehead. My heart was skipping beats. Looking into my eyes as he held my hands, he said you are the best thing that has happened to me. Emotions filled my body. I had never felt so special, so wanted, so worthy. Because of the way he made me feel, I wanted to be with him forever. It was official, I found my forever. I never wanted that moment to end. Little did he know he was the best thing that had ever happened to me too.

A loud bunch of kids entered the school and it was our cue to leave.

On our way back, we stopped at the school to see if our friends were still there but they had left. We continued to walk to the Playia where we would eventually meet up with everyone. When Julia saw us, I noticed she looked down at our hands. When she saw they were clasped together, her face did not hide her excitement! She was genuinely happy for me and I was thankful for her friendship.

The crew was hungry and all decided to go up to the restaurant to get souvlakias. Alex and I went and sat on a bench alone together. We held each other close. I didn't want to let go. His embrace felt too good. He makes me feel so good. The way he touches me and looks at me is truly like nothing I have ever experienced before. I get weak in the knees looking at him. His laugh! Oh, how I love his laugh!

His cousin came over to us and said she was freezing cold and wanted to leave. I was anything but freezing cold. In fact, I was pretty sure I was overheating. Before he left, he asked me if I wanted to go to a café in Lixouri with him tomorrow night. Our first date! I was ecstatic. Trying desperately not to look as giddy as a little school girl, I replied, I would love to. He said he would pick me up at nine-thirty p.m. He gave me a kiss that left me wanting so much more. With that, we said goodnight.

Wondering how in the world I was going to sleep tonight, I headed home. One day at a time, I thought to myself.

As I lay in bed I couldn't stop thinking about the many, many times I've already wanted to make sweet love to this man. I could feel it with every fibre of my being. However, I had made a promise to myself at a young age I would wait until I was married before consummating any relationship with intercourse. Would I be strong enough to keep this promise to myself? Only time would tell.

July 28th, 1999

This morning when I woke up, I knew I wanted to go to Lixouri. Mikey and his friend Anthi said they wouldn't mind coming along so we took the eleven o'clock bus.

When we arrived, I headed right to the internet café. I wanted to see if Shannon emailed me and also, I had so much to fill her in on. It turned out she did email me, but it was to tell me our friend had been in a serious car accident. My heart ached. These were the kinds of situations where being halfway around the world made me feel completely helpless. At this point, Shannon wasn't able to give me much more info as she herself was waiting to hear more details. I couldn't believe it. I was so sad and hoped she would be okay. I didn't feel right filling her in on the excitement I had been experiencing here, so I kept my message solely on our friend and sent my thoughts and prayers for a speedy recovery. We visited a few different stores in Lixouri before we left on the one-thirty p.m. bus back to the village.

My sweet Yiayia had lunch ready for us when we arrived back home. Right before we were going to eat, Katerina called and asked if I could go to her house. I quickly ate and hit the road.

Katerina wanted all the details of my night with Alex. She listened so intently to everything I was saying. She then told me she and Kosta saw us kiss at the Playia. I was giddy but also exhausted. I lay down in hopes of getting a little sleep before my big date! Katerina and Mikey played on the computer while I tried to sleep. Who was I kidding? I couldn't sleep! All I could think about was Alex. I laid there until seven-thirty and decided it was time to go to Yiayia's house to get ready.

Katerina, Anna and I waited for him at the Playia. I was nervous, excited and scared all at once. I had never been on a motorcycle before! I had no idea what to expect. I felt like it would be rather dangerous.

It was nine-thirty p.m. and I heard the sound of his motorcycle coming up through the village, right on time. I had a pit in my stomach. I was even more nervous than I thought I would be. Honestly, motorcycles scared the shit out of me. He looked sexy as hell riding it but I wasn't convinced about how safe it would be for me to also be on it with him. Nevertheless, unbeknownst to me, Katerina wanted to speak with him. She candidly laid out the rules; no speeding, be careful, don't bring her back too late and lastly, she told him to go wait for me at the school in the next village because my uncle was at Pavlo's and he'd see me with him if we left from there.

Pavlo's is a little variety store in our village. It's the first building you see coming into our village and the last stop going out. Older Greek men in the village gather outside to chatter. Alex graciously accepted her rules and complied. Ten minutes after he left, we left to go meet him. There he was, waiting for me, looking incredibly sexy.

He took time to explain how to get on the motorcycle and where to keep my feet. He also let me know what not to do while the bike was in motion. I found his confidence to be powerfully sexy. Timid, I got on the back of the motorcycle. Our bodies were so close together. I had my arms wrapped tightly around his waist. It felt perfect.

On our way to Lixouri, he told me he wanted to take me to the ocean. I almost died when he told me this. I've dreamed about going to the ocean with the man of my dreams. I secretly wanted to forego our café date and head straight to the beach.

Once in Lixouri, we found ourselves at a quaint little spot called L.A. The lights were dim. The music wasn't too loud or *too soft. There were only a few other people in the café. It was rather intimate. We ordered two chocolate milkshakes which were served in tall, diner-style fancy glasses. With R.E.M's Losing my Religion playing in the background, looking deep into my eyes, Alex told me that before he met me everything in his life was going wrong. He held my hands close to his body, as he continued to say that when we met, he felt it was like magic. I could feel every word he was saying so deep into my bones. It was exactly how I felt. I knew the magic, magnetic spark I felt had to have been mutual, so hearing him say it in his own words made it even more incredible. It was such great validation for how I was feeling.*

Hand in hand, we took a stroll to the pier. I had also been dying to walk this long pier with him. There was something so romantic about it, especially at night. Surrounded by the beauty of the water as we walked to the end of the pier, I was admiring the glow of the lights. You could see all of the Lixouri and Argostoli lights shining so perfectly. We sat and held one another. Feeling his soft kisses graze my neck gave me goosebumps. He was always so tender and careful. We couldn't stop kissing one another. He whispered in my ear he wanted to take me to the beach. To which I responded, tonight? He had mentioned it earlier but I assumed he meant another night, for another date. No, he meant tonight. It was difficult to contain my excitement. Was this real life? I felt like I was living in a fairytale. I was speechless. My manifestation skills were on point.

The gooseneck lights lining the pier led our way back. We found where we left his motorcycle and headed to the beach. In my body, I felt giddy excitement and a strong desire to continue exploring our magnetic connection.

We arrived around midnight. It was as magical as one could imagine. We took our shoes off and walked hand in hand down the beach, feeling the cold sand between our toes, until we found the perfect spot to settle into. He sat behind me with his arms wrapped around me. My head rested on his firm chest. I could feel his breath against my neck. It was incredibly romantic. Listening to the sound of the waves crashing onto the sand, watching the sparkle of the stars as the full moon gave the most beautiful glow on the ocean. It was truly breathtaking.

Admittedly, we didn't stay in that position long. Our bodies weaved together as we passionately explored one another in many different positions. His body on top of mine, my hands gently reached toward his shirt, lifting it and taking it off. The smell of his body and the taste of his lips were intoxicating. Alternating between kissing my top and bottom lip, each of his movements were skilled and seductive. It felt as though we were in slow motion – him feeling every single inch of my body, and me feeling his. The build-up to this moment was so intense I could barely believe it was happening. I wasn't nervous at all. I was taking in every second of this euphoric, divinely orchestrated experience.

I adored the way he would glimpse at me with his sexy eyes, while his mouth and hands were driving my body wild. My shirt was now off and in the chill of the ocean air, I felt the heat of his mouth as he kissed his way up my toned stomach. I let out soft moans as the warmth of his hands caressed my hard nipples. I had never felt such ecstasy. In his arms, I felt so safe and wildly desired. We lay on the beach until three-thirty in the morning. It took a lot of strength to resist making sweet love to him there on that beach.

The pieces of my heart that struggled so deeply to find love and connection felt like they were being glued together sitting there in his warm embrace. Because of him, I felt far away from the sad, lonely girl I once was. The girl, who in ninth grade, was called Bert and Ernie (from Sesame Street), on the school bus because of my thick, connecting eyebrows. I was far away from the girl who sat terrified as clementines were being thrown at me from the seats behind. Beautiful wasn't ever the word I used to describe myself. If I could have only seen my beauty then. More so, if I could have only seen my inner beauty and allowed myself to feel proud. Instead, I let their cruel words and actions dictate my self-worth.

In these, our most tender moments, despite my inability to speak Greek fluently and his inability to speak fluent English, our connection – in its truest, most authentic form – was flourishing. The language was irrelevant. We were able to communicate far beyond what words could ever say. With my arms wrapped around his waist, there wasn't enough room for a piece of paper between us. I enjoyed his aroma while kissing his neck as we rode back to the village. Him riding the motorcycle, and me riding the high. This sweet ecstasy must be what heaven feels like. Sweet dreams were made of nights like these.

Chapter 9

July 29, 1999

I was half asleep when I heard the phone ringing. It seemed as though it would not stop. I was too tired to get out of bed, but I felt like it might be important. I quickly glanced at the clock as I ran to answer. It was ten-thirty a.m. My cousin Kosta was on the other end and he did not sound happy with me. He asked me what time I got home last night and then told me he would speak to me about it later and hung up. I realized it was late, but what was it to him? My dad was back in Canada, and I sure wasn't accepting applications for a new one here.

Not only was he upset with me, but Katerina also would not speak to me.

I didn't think going to the beach was going to be an option for me today, especially not Petani. But as the universe would have it, I found myself there this afternoon thanks to my friend Julia.

Not long after I arrived, I saw Kosta speaking to Alex. I was so angry. I am pretty sure steam was coming out of my ears. Immediately, I looked away. Instead, I stared at the ocean, focusing my attention on ripples and waves. Feeling the ocean breeze against my flushed skin helped to calm me. I started to feel my breath again and my heart rate began to simmer. Niko came to ask if I wanted to play racquetball with him. I loved playing, so I graciously accepted his offer. We played for a while before it was time to go.

I couldn't leave without speaking to him. I was nervous as I walked toward the restaurant. My heart began beating faster. My eyes looked down while thoughts raced in my head.

I hoped he wasn't upset with me. Our eyes met and I quickly felt relief. The restaurant was full of people. I knew he was busy and I didn't want to be a bother. I asked if he was coming to see me tonight. He said yes. With that, we smiled at one another. His bright smile and irresistible wink left me wanting him, every bit of him.

Getting ready for his arrival tonight, I couldn't help but think of how lucky I am. I stared in the mirror, noticing how my eyes were twinkling and my smile was so authentic. I feel as though he is my Prince Charming and my life is like a fairytale.

I met up with a bunch of the girls around nine-thirty p.m. and we all went up to the restaurant to get something to eat. The food here is delicious. I felt a special connection with Julia. She was always so kind, positive and her smile lit up the room. I enjoyed our friendship and felt grateful to have met her. Our laughter and conversation filled the dining room as the delicious food filled our bellies.

Alex arrived around eleven p.m. Hearing the sound of his motorcycle and seeing his face brought me more joy than anything ever had before. Every time, my heart skipped a beat and butterflies filled my stomach.

We all decided to go to Pí-ye, which was a couple of villages away. My uncle and his friends were at Pavlo's, so that meant the girls and I would leave first. I was giddy the whole walk there. I couldn't wait to spend time with him. We were there for about ten minutes before he arrived. We all gathered around chatting. It wasn't long before Alex and I excused ourselves for some alone time together.

Walking hand in hand, we found a quiet place to sit together with a beautiful view. We kissed a lot. Oh, did I love kissing him. I wish I could spend a whole day and night kissing him. His lips were silky soft. He was gentle but in a powerful, masculine way. In the darkness, I could see his face in the moonlight. My heart was pounding. I sat there, feeling desire and utter arousal run from my heart, to my chest, and toward my inner thighs. My body was heating up. Slow, soft kisses mixed with faster kissing and some light lip biting. His fingers lightly touched the nape of my neck, and as he moved my hair away it gave me goosebumps. His fingers continued to run down my shoulders to my hands. He held my hands gently, yet firm, and put them in front of me and paused. I felt safe. My heart was about to beat out of my chest. I closed my eyes and took a deep breath out. I felt the intensity flood my body and the rhythmic pulsing down there had me weak in the knees. We stared into each other's eyes. No words were spoken or needed. In his eyes, I felt love, protection, happiness, and respect. Leaning my head on his chest, with his arms wrapped around me, I didn't want him to ever let go.

July 31, 1999

Today did not start as a great day. I went to see Katerina but she was still upset with me and wouldn't talk to me. It's starting to make me angry. I get it, I was late getting home that night. She was worried and I can appreciate that. However, I am an adult!

I went home and made my favourite snack, a piece of french bread drizzled in olive oil with a squeezed tomato on top garnished with sea salt. I ate four pieces. Emotional eating at its finest. I was at home by myself with nothing to do, so I went back to sleep. I was exhausted anyway.

A few hours later, I called to see if Kosta was going to Space tonight. Katerina answered the phone. I knew this conversation would not end well as soon as she heard my voice. It didn't stop me from at least asking her if she was going to Space tonight. It was a hard no. I didn't expect a different answer from her but I guess I was hoping Kosta would have answered the phone instead.

I was bummed. But I was determined. Some way, somehow, I would get to Space tonight. As I was wallowing in my sorrows, I got a surprise visit from Julia. She came in, and I made her a frappé. We were having a great conversation and then she asked if I wanted to go to Space with her and Eleni. Did I? 1000%. Thank you Universe!

We left my grandparents' home and went to hers to get ready for the night ahead. She was so sweet, when we arrived at her house. She made me a sandwich and then showed me how the shower worked. It didn't take me long to get ready to go, hair, makeup and all.

Making our way into the centre of the town, we met up with some more friends of ours. We took a walk down the pier. It was different walking the pier without him. I hadn't seen him yet. I was concerned I had missed him at the café. Gina was with my friends and I. We had spoken a few times since that awful day I left her house. I had told her about Alex, and she was excited for me and wanted to meet him. I tried to be present with the girls, but I couldn't stop thinking about him.

Walking back from the pier I saw him sitting at an outdoor café with his friends. As soon as he saw me, he promptly stood up and came to meet me. He looked gorgeous, as usual. He introduced me to everyone at the table, including his stunning sister, Sophia.

Gina grabbed my attention and whispered in my ear, "Wow, you sure can pick 'em." We shared a big smile. I was proud, he really was amazing.

As we sat at the café, Alex leaned over and whispered in my ear, "You look beautiful," then he asked if I wanted to go for a walk to the pier. He had a way of always making me feel so special in any and every situation. We stayed at the pier for half an hour. It looked different when I was there with him. The lights shone brighter, the air was warmer, and the smells were sweeter.

To think of how much has changed in the last two weeks is pretty incredible. I went from wanting the next flight out to finding my soulmate less than twenty-four hours later. It's been amazing. I definitely have a grateful heart tonight.

We met back up with our friends. I went with the girls to Space and he met me there. Holy shit, the vodka drinks are strong. I swear half the glass was vodka with a splash of orange juice.

The club was electric tonight. We slipped in among the crowd, ready to move to the music. I felt the vibe and let my body go free. Feeling every beat and ounce of sweat. It all felt so good.

It was around three a.m. and he took my hand and guided me outside to the balcony. It was one of the most gorgeous, picturesque views I had ever seen. Pictures would not be able to do the view justice. Looking deep into each other's eyes, I ran my nails gently up and down his back over his dress shirt. It drove him crazy and he told me how good it made him feel. Making out with him in front of such a spectacular backdrop added to the romance. He kept telling me how beautiful I was. He certainly knew how to awaken my inner goodness. Our bodies grew tight in alignment. I could feel through his pants he was hard as a rock. It felt good knowing I made him feel that way. I wished he could feel how good he made me feel too. He couldn't at that moment, but I knew he could see it in my eyes.

August 1, 1999

I can hardly believe it's August already! Where has the time gone? Katerina is still upset with me. I'm not sure why she is being so stubborn. I hope she gets over it soon. It wasn't like us to not speak for so long. Maybe something else was upsetting her too.

Around eleven p.m, two of Alex's friends came to my village and found me at the Playia. They wanted to tell me he would be there in half an hour. He sent messengers! How sweet was that?

Half an hour later, my love had arrived. We sat on a bench facing the ocean. It was late but the view with lights was still beautiful. We were waiting for a few other people to come. The plan was for all of us to go to the old school. He held me until they arrived. Then I had to go with them so that my uncle didn't suspect anything. Outrageous. I could buy them cigarettes and alcohol when I was seven, but I couldn't have a boyfriend as an adult.

We stopped at Pavlo's to wait for Elena's boyfriend. I couldn't wait any longer. I went to the school to be with Alex. He wasn't there. I walked back to our group. They said maybe he went to the school in Rifi. I let them know I would catch up with them later and I made my way to Rifi.

As I approached the school, I could see his shadow in the dark. He was sitting on his motorcycle waiting. When he saw me, he started walking toward me, but not casually. He was speed walking. When he reached me, he put his hands on my cheeks and passionately kissed me. I saw this happen in the movies a thousand times and I never thought it would be something I would be lucky enough to experience. It is with these little actions he made me feel so loved. I cannot believe how fortunate I am to have met and fallen in love with this man.

August 2, 1999
Today, a well-known Greek singer is coming to our village to perform. Vasilis Lekkas was set to hit the stage. After I plucked, shaved, primped and primed I headed to the Playia. It was nine p.m. and it was packed full. It was an exciting event to have a musician come to our little village. I was wearing a long, lacy black dress I had bought in Argostoli this morning. I was able to spot Elena and Alexandra as they weren't in the huge crowd of people. We chatted a bit and then I had two messengers come to tell me Alex was at the school waiting for me. My heart started to beat faster. That feeling never got old.

Tonight, I could really feel the coolness in the air as I made my way to him. I knew once we were together, I would forget about how cold I was. We were so happy to see one another. We went into the school and sat on a set of stairs. At last, now we were shielded from the wind but I was confident it would get pretty hot in there.

We began kissing. Oh, I loved kissing him. He was a great kisser. When we kiss it feels like time stops. My body lit on fire with each graze of his tongue, each gentle bite on my lips and the tender way he stroked my hair. I loved the way he held me so close to his body.

Damn it. We were interrupted by a bunch of rowdy kids. I didn't want to leave, but we couldn't stay there any longer. Also, it was late so Alex drove me home. We shared a sweet goodnight kiss. He gave me that wink of his that made me melt and off he went.

August 4, 1999

Kosta took us to Petani to swim today. We didn't go to the big part of the beach, but rather to the little part off to the right side. It didn't have the same appeal since I wasn't able to feast my eyes on my love. It was driving me crazy, so I made my way to the other side of the beach. The restaurant he worked in was very busy. However, that didn't stop him from taking time to see me. He even brought me my favourite drink, a peach iced tea. We shared a smile and a quick exchange of words and then Kosta came to pick me up. I was sad to leave but I knew I would be seeing him later tonight.

When he arrived at ten-thirty p.m, we all went to Pí-ye; Katerina, Elena, Nikos, Mikey, Vangelis and Giannis, Alex and I. It was about a twenty-five-minute walk. The crew stayed about forty-five minutes and then they all left. It was the two of us left there together.

We were in a secluded area with the night sky aglow. In the distance, the city lights of Argostoli twinkled. We looked up at the blanket of stars that seemed to stretch to infinity.

I couldn't have felt more comfortable in his embrace. It was silent. He put his hand to my chin and guided my face toward his. He studied my face with his eyes, tracing my jawline with his fingers. Looking into my eyes he said, "I love you." My body *froze. The moment felt surreal. Smiling as my eyes became glossy, I told him I loved him too. We shared many more tender, sweet kisses snuggled so closely. I couldn't get enough of him. I was enthralled. Three weeks exactly from the day we met. Three. Another sign from the Universe?*

We stayed cuddled up, enjoying one another for quite a while. It felt amazing. At one-fifteen a.m, we began to walk toward my village. Another luscious kiss goodnight and a promise to see one another tomorrow.

August 5, 1999
Katerina, Kosta, Giannis and I went to Agia Eleni today. It was a sweltering hot day. Katerina and I laid our towels over the little rocks that filled the beach.

As we worked on our tans, I caught her up on the latest news between Alex and I. She seemed to be happy for me. My eyes closed, soaking up the sun, and suddenly I was picked up and thrown into the ocean. Kosta and Giannis thought I needed to cool down. I couldn't be mad, it felt refreshing. After laughing, Katerina came in too.

We pretended we were synchronized swimmers. I'm sure it appeared more like we were dancing trying not to drown. It was pretty hilarious. We left the beach at five-thirty p.m. I was going to stay at Gina's house for a few days and needed to prepare.

Gina and I met Alex where the boats come in at ten-thirty p.m. He looked strikingly handsome. Many times, I wondered how I got so darn lucky.

The three of us took a walk to the pier. From a distance, I saw his sister walking toward us. She only joined us briefly. Still, it was nice to see her.

Alex, Gina and I left and went to a café in the square. As we sat, Alex enjoyed a Heineken, Gina a vodka and me, a peach juice. Alcohol made me tired so I gave myself permission to not have to drink it. Lord knows I could have a great time without it. I'm sure Gina felt much like a third wheel. It didn't seem to bother her though. We were happy to spend time with her.

We decided to go for a walk. Gina wanted to go for a walk by herself and I wasn't going to stop her. I was itching for some alone time with my love. I was craving his sweet kisses on my lips. It didn't take us long to erupt into fast and slow kissing. We were insatiable. Though it was getting late. Gina and I needed to be at her Theia's house by two a.m. I told him I hated to leave him, he said he hated to leave me as well. With that, we kissed goodnight and off I went.

August 6, 1999

Today, it hit me. I realized I would be leaving Alex in two weeks. I felt tears welling up in my eyes. I cried uncontrollably. I couldn't bear to think about this summer coming to an end and what it was going to be like to leave him.

What would happen to our relationship? Would he wait for me? My thoughts swirled as I cried into the pillow. Gina came in and helped me settle down. Somehow, I managed to get to a place of calm. I needed to focus on the precious time we had and try not to worry about what was out of my control.

Alex and I met up in Lixouri and went for our usual walk down the pier. I was trying not to be emotional. Cuddling and kissing him, I knew I wanted to savour every single moment together.

We made plans to meet up with Gina and Peter tonight. Peter is one of Alex's best friends on the island. We met them at the square. A large crowd filled the centre as live Greek music provided entertainment, but there were no empty chairs. It forced us out of our usual outdoor café and into a brick and mortar one. We headed up the stairs and sat on the balcony of the high building. I loved the view overlooking the water and the pier. We could watch as the large boats came and went.

After finishing up our drinks, Gina and Peter wanted to go to another bar. Alex and I decided to go back to the pier. It had quickly become our happy place.

This time was a little different. Our connection was more involved, you could say. Hot and heavy kissing lead to hot and heavy touching and massaging of each other's bodies. I felt completely aroused. I was intoxicated by him. We couldn't get enough of each other. Watching him admire my chest with his eyes turned me on. He gently squeezed my nipple, it felt like an electric spark that spanned far beyond my chest. With his other hand caressing the nape of my neck and up into my hair, goosebumps filled my body. With all the sensations together, I had feelings in my body I had never experienced before. I knew it would be like a drug that I needed more of. A lot more.

August 7, 1999

This morning I was hoping to take the bus from Lixouri to our village to get some things I needed. I had bought a new dress I wanted to wear and I still needed underwear and a few personal hygiene items. When I got to where the buses were, they let me know there was only one bus that went to my village and I had already missed it. I guess I had time to finish shopping, so I went to a periptero (news agent's shop) in the square to use a payphone to call Gina. I wanted to ask if she wanted to join me. She did.

While out I found a really cute black mini skirt and a crop top that looked great on me. I also found a pair of underwear. Twenty dollars for a pair of knickers! I couldn't believe it. I mean, they were nice but that price tag seemed to be a little excessive. Back home I could get at least five pairs for that amount of money. There is no doubt they would be very admired, so I let it go and bought the underwear.

After we were done shopping, Gina and I went back to her Theia's house. She had prepared Yemista for us and it was so good. Everyone here can cook. The food is out of this world. We had an afternoon nap, which by the way, I now appreciated more than ever before.

Plucking my eyebrows, we chatted about how our evening would go. Gina really liked Peter and he really liked her. We were going to meet Alex and Peter where the boats dock. We planned to take the ten-thirty p.m. ferry to Argostoli. We were both giddy and excited for the night to begin.

We walked into town and headed to where the boats came in. We were giddy as we stood there waiting for our Greek gods to arrive. Looking mighty dapper, there they were. We walked up to the second deck of the ferry. Gina and Peter took a seat across from Alex and I. The view on the boat was spectacular. There was something so romantic about nighttime.

Argostoli was bustling with people everywhere. It was hard to believe, especially given the time of night it was. We couldn't find a seat in their city centre. Finally, a little table opened up at a sweet little ice cream shoppe. I did love ice cream, that was no secret. I had my favourite chocolate ice cream in a cone, Alex and Peter had a chocolate and strawberry mix and Gina had a milkshake. It was a quick trip over. We just wanted something different to pass the time before we went to Space.

My eye caught the beauty of my cousin Afroditi when we got to the club. She was with her boyfriend, Dionysis. I was able to introduce her to Alex. Afroditi was a few years older than me. I had always felt a special connection to her from a very young age. I was proud to be able to introduce such an incredible man to her.

Alex and I only stayed for a little while. He asked me if I wanted to go back to Lixouri to our favourite spot, the pier. I couldn't get out of the club fast enough.

It's funny because no matter where we are, it seems someone was always around. It was three a.m. and there was a fisherman a few feet from us. Who the hell goes finishing in a rowboat at three a.m? It made us giggle. We just adjusted. We climbed over the rock wall that lined the pier and sat on the other side.

Nothing could stop our hungry hearts. It was another night full of passion as kissing commenced. My awareness was brought to my chest as I felt both of his warm hands cupping my breasts. His hands were powerful yet so gentle. Simultaneously feeling his breath while he kissed and nibbled my neck was electrifying. I couldn't help but let out a few moans in complete and utter pleasure.

I was craving his body. I wanted to feel his bare skin against mine. Unbuttoning his shirt, revealed his chest. It was like a piece of artwork I had long desired. Perfectly sculpted with the right amount of chest hair. He was without a doubt, manly. I found him fiercely sexy.

I wanted to devour his body. Hearing him moan as I licked and sucked his nipples drove me wild. He slid his hand down, making slow circular motions over my panties. I could feel the heat and moistness between my legs. He went from kissing my lips to my neck, to my breasts, around my stomach and down to where his hands were. Feeling him kiss me there was indescribable. It was the most intense, incredible feeling. Every stroke of his tongue moved with such intention and deep passion. The sensations of him touching me all over my body, holding me so close to him was more than a dream come true. I never knew this kind of pleasure existed. More than anything, I didn't want this time together to end.

Unfortunately, we had to head back to Space. Gina would be looking for us as it was four-fifteen a.m.

Getting ready for bed, we couldn't stop talking. I was happy she and Peter had a great night as well. We concluded tonight was the best night yet.

Chapter 10

August 8, 1999

Today, the heat was exhausting. Gina and I stayed in our beds most of the day. I slept a lot, trying to recover. When I wasn't sleeping, I was enjoying vivid flashbacks of last night.

Alex met me in Lixouri at ten-thirty p.m. As soon as I saw him, I could tell something was wrong. I had an immediate pit in my stomach. It was a quiet walk to the pier. My stomach was in knots. We sat down and looked into each other's eyes. I told him that I felt something was wrong and asked if he wanted to talk about it. He said his best friend is upset with him because he is always coming to see me and feels as though he doesn't want to be around him anymore because he has me.

Then the conversation took a turn. For some reason I said, "What if when I go back to Canada you find another girl?"

He responded with, "What if you find another man?" I made it clear there was no one else in this whole world for me. He was it. The conversation continued.

I looked at my watch and realized it was twelve-fifteen a.m. and I had to be back to Gina's Theia's house by twelve-thirty or she would be upset. I let him know we had to leave. He was trying to give me different scenarios to help me understand what he was saying. I wasn't understanding. I was getting visibly upset. He looked at me and said, "I love you." I returned the sentiment. I wanted to hold him forever.

We got on his motorcycle and left the pier. My heart was shaking the whole way to Gina's. When we arrived, he wanted some more time to speak with me. I wanted to be respectful of Gina's Theia, so I went inside the house to ask if it would be okay if I stayed outside the door for ten minutes. She gave me the green light and for that I was thankful.

We sat down, he looked into my eyes and said, "Do you know how much I love you? You are the first woman I have ever said I love you to." He proceeded to tell me I had his heart in my hands and not to throw it away.

Initially, I was confused. I didn't realize he thought I was questioning his love for me or questioning if in fact I loved him too. I said, "Go home and get some sleep."

He said, "Who needs sleep?"

I said, "You do!"

He said, "I don't need sleep, I need you." My heart melted. We kissed again. The tenderness of his kiss and the passion behind it tugged at my soul. He held me in his arms as we shared a few more kisses, then, sadly, it was time to say goodnight.

August 11, 1999

Tonight, I was alone in my village, waiting at the Playia for Alex to come. I could hear his motorcycle coming through the village. I felt a surge through my body. His motorcycle had a very distinctive sound, at least to my ears. I'm not sure if it was the way he drove it or the motorcycle itself, or both? I could also hear he wasn't alone. Another motorcycle was with him. A bit surprised, I wondered who he was with.

Alex arrived with his best friend. He greeted me with a kiss and then asked me if I wanted to go to a beach party. There was no way my uncle was going to allow me to go to a beach party this late at night. But it didn't stop me from asking. Again, I put my persuasive pants on and somehow convinced him to let me go. He thought all the girls from the village were going. That truly was my intent, it just didn't work out that way. Friends had already made plans and to be fair it was late and very last minute.

While we were at the beach waiting for everyone to arrive, we laid down together. We asked how each other's day was and how yesterday was as we didn't see one another. He told me I was like his drug and that he needed to have me. I felt the exact same way.

We started to build a little house out of rocks on the beach. It was the sweetest thing ever as we described each room and who would occupy them, referring to our kids someday.

When the others arrived, Alex helped Petros start a fire. The fire was sizzling. The crackle and hiss and the beauty of the night stars set the tone for the evening. Alex's mom and dad came to the beach for a short visit. It was nice to spend time with them. As they were leaving, his mom rubbed my arm and said goodnight. She was so sweet. From the gleam in her eyes and the smile on her face, she made me feel as though I had her stamp of approval.

We laughed, sang and danced around the crackling of fire, with our friends, into the early hours of the morning. All night, Alex and I held each other's gaze, looking deep into each other's eyes. Our connection was incredible. I feel like I'm in heaven when I'm with him. Nothing could make me happier.

August 15, 1999
Tonight, Alex picked me up from my village. We were going to spend the night in Lixouri. First, he needed to stop at his house to get his license.

When his mother saw me, she immediately stood, came toward me and with a big embrace, kissed both of my cheeks. His dad followed suit. I was so surprised. They made me feel very welcome in their home. His mom introduced me to their guests as their son's girlfriend. She then brought me sweets and a glass of water. Thankfully, she didn't bring a "spoon sweet," that would have been awkward. His parents are lovely. I can see how much love their family has for one another. It's heartwarming.

We went back to our usual spot in Lixouri, the pier. Many people were out walking the pier. Sounds ranged from laughter to silence as people passed by. We both enjoyed people watching. We started talking about what we would do when I had to go back to Canada. It was sad and depressing to think about. I tried hard to avoid it, but as the days were getting closer it was becoming all I could think about.

We stopped talking and started kissing. We wanted to touch every single part of each other. And we did. It felt incredible. With his magical fingers, he had me moaning all night long. Somehow, I managed to keep my virginity. But honestly, I don't know how much longer I can I was taken to an alternate universe. One I didn't want to come back from.

There never seemed to be enough time with him. I looked at my watch, it was three-thirty a.m. How was it possible for hours to vanish? I knew we had to go. He felt bad we lost track of time.

We kissed all the way back down the pier to his bike. We were like magnets. Our bodies couldn't be apart from one another. I felt bad because he was so worried. He knew what I had experienced the last time I came home so late. He didn't want me to go through that again. He was trying so hard to think of what he would say if they were waiting for me. His lips were warm and soft. I could feel and smell his sweet breath under my nose. We parted our lips slightly, allowing our tongues to dance one last time for the night.

Walking toward the house I saw all the lights on. My heart dropped. I envisioned my uncle waiting as I opened the door, ready to lose his mind on me. I had to think quickly. Instead of going in the front door, I headed to the back of the house and climbed through my bedroom window. I couldn't believe I did that. I felt like such a badass. Once in, I looked over at Katerina's bed, it was empty. I lay there for about five minutes trying to think of what I should do.

With my heart racing, I decided to go out into the kitchen. Much to my surprise, Mikey and Katerina were sitting on the couch. To say I was relieved was an understatement. I told them what I had done and we all had a good laugh. She wanted to know all about my night. I wasn't ready to tell her everything, so I modified and told her just a little. She asked me if I wanted to go up to the Playia. I was shocked, but of course I was up for it. Out the window we climbed and headed to the Playia. We were surprised that a few of our friends were there. It was four-thirty a.m.

We were exhausted and decided to go back home. We climbed back through our bedroom window and laughed hysterically. Tonight was an incredible night.

August 16, 1999
Needless to say, I slept the day away. My body needed to recover from the many, many late nights.

It was around nine-thirty p.m. when Katerina and I went up to the Playia. I was wearing my Campus Crew pants with my red Ikeda sweater, black lace bra and no underwear.

Alex usually came around ten-thirty but it was eleven-thirty and still no sign of him. I was getting worried, thinking the worst. It was not a good feeling. Thankfully, it wasn't much longer before he had arrived.

As soon as I saw him, I jumped up and ran over to kiss him. It was a combination of relief and my excitement to see him that made that moment feel so good. I could tell by the smile on his face that he was equally as happy to see me.

As the Playia started to fill in with friends and others, Katerina told us to go back to the windmill to have some alone time together. She was so sweet. She knew the looming date was getting closer and closer. I appreciated her thoughtful suggestion.

Aside from its technical use, the windmill boasted a beautiful old-fashioned facade. We started out lying down beside each other, cuddling and kissing. It was dark, the ground hard and cold. I moved my body on top of his, kissing more passionately. I took off my sweater, rolled it up into a ball and placed it under his head. As his hands were massaging my back, he pressed me tight against him. In the coolness of the night, my nipples perked up with the warmth of his breath. I was trying desperately to forget the little time we had left together. I wasn't ready to leave. There was so much I wanted and needed before I left. Being alone at the bottom of this beautiful windmill was the perfect imperfect setting to explore more of his body. We were savages for each other. I truly didn't know how much longer I could keep the promise I made to myself.

I let my hard nipples glide down his body until I reached the top of his pants. Fumbling, trying my best to unzip his pants quickly, I finally felt him between my hands. My instincts took over. Feeling a little wetness, my hand began to slowly yet firmly move up and down his hard shaft. I changed my grip between firm and soft. Sexy, undiscovered territory had me steamed up and ready to explore.

As my lips grazed the tip, I felt him quiver. Getting to know his most intimate body parts with my mouth was exhilarating. Wrapping my mouth around and taking him deep down my throat sent him over the edge. I could feel him pulsing and his moans got louder. He held my hand the entire time. It was incredibly sweet and comforting. I loved being able to bring him such pleasure.

He gently laid me on my back. Watching his sexy body mount mine gave me full-body goosebumps. His lips met mine but quickly continued down my body. I felt him smoothly take my pants down to my knees. He spread my legs apart. The anticipation of what was coming could not have prepared me for what I received. It felt so intense and powerful as he thrust his tongue unhurriedly in and out of my very wet vagina. My soft breathing quickly turned into clear moans of pleasure as I experienced that unbelievable bliss. His fingers were as gentle as they were soft. He squeezed my nipples, giving me jolts of ecstasy. We were hot and heavy. Never had I felt such euphoria. He let me know he had a condom if I wanted to take things further. I hesitated. I wanted to; I really did. But I wasn't ready. It didn't feel like it was the time or the place to make love for my first time. He completely understood and remained supportive and respectful.

We shared another unforgettable night. It was perfect. He was perfect.

August 20, 1999
Tonight, Elena kept me company in the Playia while I waited for my love to arrive. The sound of his motorcycle coming through the village instantly brought a smile to my face.

He asked if I wanted to go to Lixouri for coffee. Without hesitation, I jumped on the back of his bike and wrapped my arms around him. We found a group of his friends sitting at one of the outdoor cafés. Knowing I love peaches, Alex ordered me a peach juice. We stayed a while and then took a walk to the pier.

He could tell something was bothering me. He was so sweet, compassionate and empathic. I began to bawl. Tears streamed down my face. He knew exactly what was wrong. He felt the same. He confided in me he wouldn't be able to go to my village after I left as I wouldn't be there waiting for him with a big smile on my face. Of course, I cried harder.

Amidst the tears flowing, I looked into his eyes and saw a tear making its way down his cheek. This was hard. I don't know how I will make it until next summer without him physically by my side. He was so sweetly trying to wipe my tears but he couldn't keep up.

Thinking we needed to get our minds off of what our future held, we went for a walk back to the square. We found our way to the bar we had our first date at. We had a drink and decided, given the time, it would be best to head back to my village. The reality of me leaving has hit both of us pretty hard. I'm trying my best to live in the moment and enjoy every second we have together. But it's too much.

August 21, 1999

Today, I wanted to spend some time with my Yiayia and Pappou before I leave the island tomorrow. I wanted to make sure we took some pictures together before I went back to Canada.

My grandparents are lovely people. But the reality is, they aren't going to live forever. They, of course, know how much I love them and vice versa. I am grateful for all the time I got to spend with them. The pure unconditional love they shower upon me makes me feel like a kid even though I'm an adult.

My Pappou was notorious for giving me pocket money. They shared their experiences, gave guidance and advice, always thinking of the well-being of the family and others, values and morals, dos and don'ts, culture, ethics and so much more. I realize how lucky I was to stay at their little home in the village that meant so much to them and I. I cherished them.

Tonight, when Alex arrived, he asked me if we could go on a little adventure. I wasn't turning down an adventure with him. Ready to leave Lixouri, we got on the ferry to Argostoli and then drove to a little town called Lassi.

We found the most beautiful café/bar I had ever seen. We sat down and ordered two frozen strawberry daiquiris. While we were drinking these delicious drinks, he said he had something in his pocket that was bothering him. He took out a little box that was wrapped with a bow on top and handed it to me. I was shocked. I didn't know what to do or say. The twinkle in his eyes and the smile on his face was adorable.

My heart was racing. I didn't believe he was asking me to marry him. I knew it couldn't possibly be that. I was taken aback. Excited, he told me to open the box. Inside was a beautiful heart ring. The left side was outlined in diamonds and a diamond sat in the middle of the heart. It was gorgeous and definitely unexpected. He put the ring on my finger and told me how much he loved me and how happy I made him. He couldn't believe he was so lucky to have met and fallen in love with me. We kissed.

I reached for my purse and took out a box for him to open. He looked just as surprised as I was. He opened the box and found a ring. I told him I felt the exact same way about him, as he did for me.

It was wild to me that we both got each other a ring without knowing the other had done the same. It was our promise to each other. We didn't need a ring to solidify our relationship or the commitment we had for one another because we were madly in love with one another. The rings were a beautiful symbol.

After finishing our drinks and ice cream, we left the café. Walking hand in hand around Lassi was romantic. It was a very quaint village. As we walked, Alex asked if I would be up for going to Space. His friends were going to be there and he thought it might be nice for us to all be together before I left. I couldn't say no as long as I got to be with him.

The club was busy, people were everywhere. The beat of the music hit my ears a little differently tonight. I had a few drinks and all of a sudden it was four-thirty a.m.

We left the club and headed back to my village. He dropped me off at the Playia. We looked deep into each other's eyes before he had to go. We kissed goodnight. I couldn't say anything. I just cried.

He started to drive away, but he quickly turned around and asked if I wanted to sit with him on a bench. He always knew exactly what I needed. Truthfully, I didn't want to ever leave him, but at that moment I would take a seat on a bench with him.

We kissed as I cried, and cried, on his shoulder. He held me so tenderly as he softly kissed my forehead. It was really late. It was almost morning and he had to work in just a few hours. I had to let him leave.

I made my way back to my bed, and cried myself to sleep.

August 22, 1999

I cried all day today. Katerina, Mikey, Theia Maria and I played one last game of Ace to King together. I packed all of my things and left the village, headed to Lixouri.

Getting out the door without tears was impossible. My heart was hurting. Why did I have to live so far from Greece?

My next stop was to see my grandparents. I tried to be strong. I was about as strong as a mouse in front of cheese. I saw my grandfather start to cry and that did me in. I thought about how this could be the last time we see one another, to hug, to say I love you. They were getting older and their health was not the greatest.

Katerina had come up to our grandparents' house with me. We were trying to squeeze every last second together. She was crying, I was crying. This summer we had all spent a lot of time together. We were closer than we had ever been. With tears in our eyes, we hugged goodbye, promising to email as often as we could. With that, Theia Maria and Theo Stavros brought me to Gina's house in Lixouri.

Standing in her kitchen, I cried more. I couldn't believe our time here was over. This would be my last night with Alex until next summer.

I met him at the square in Lixouri at ten p.m. He was never late. When he arrived, I jumped onto the back of his motorcycle and ripped the slit in my brand new skirt.

He took me to the pier for a short time before he took me back to his house to say goodbye to his parents and sister. His parents were very hospitable. Making sure we had something to drink and eat. Sitting around their kitchen table, his mom showed me pictures of Alex as a baby. He was an absolute gem. So adorable.

Then tears started to roll down her cheeks. She was sad because I was leaving. She confided in me that she thought I was a very good girl and that she loved me. My heart sank. I couldn't control the tears flowing from my eyes. She gave me six hugs while we both continued to cry. Much to my surprise, his dad also had tears in his eyes. It was so difficult saying goodbye to these beautiful souls. There were no words for how good it felt to be loved and accepted by his family. I was over the moon. He was my person.

After we left his parents' home, he took me to his cousin's restaurant. It wasn't far and we didn't stay long. We enjoyed some ice cream. He certainly knew how to soothe my hurting heart.

It was late at night and the restaurant was fairly empty. He looked at me and said, "Think of something in your mind and I'll tell you what you are thinking."

I smiled and said, "Okay." While looking into his hypnotic eyes, I said, "I love you" in my mind over, and over, and over again.

After about thirty seconds, he looked deep into my eyes and said, "I love you too."

I was shocked. My jaw dropped. I could have been thinking anything. It was my last night with him, I could have been thinking about how I don't want to leave. How did he know? There was something to be said about how special and unique our bond was.

He asked me where I wanted to go next. It didn't matter to me, as long as we were together. As we drove through Lixouri, I held him tight. I wondered where we were going. He took me to a beach we hadn't been to before.

For both of us, the water was so calming and beautiful. We took all of our clothes off. We needed to feel each other's bodies one last time. I told him I wanted to make love to him so badly, but I couldn't. Not yet. We both wanted it more than anything. He was very understanding and compassionate about my desire to wait. It definitely didn't dampen the mood.

We took care of each other's bodies, made love without needing to have intercourse. Anytime we spent together was magical. I can't even begin to imagine what it will be like to make love to this man.

The sound of the waves in the background as we explored and excited every part of one another's body added to the romance. I never imagined I would have the ability to feel so damn good. He is absolutely incredible. The love, care, tenderness and magic he shows me every single day is amazing. I truly feel like the luckiest person in the entire world.

As much as I wished we could have stayed at that beach forever, we couldn't. It was four-thirty a.m. and I needed to get to Gina's house.

On the back of the motorcycle, wrapping my arms around his body so tightly I burst into tears. I realized these would be our final minutes together for a very long time. I wasn't ready to say goodbye. I felt our romance was just getting started.

We promised one another we would write and call as often as we could. With our tears, runny noses and broken hearts we stood under the moonlight embracing and kissing non-stop.

This experience had been the most incredible one of my life. Meeting and falling in love with this man had been nothing short of magical.

As my head hit the pillow one last time on this island, I cried myself to sleep.

Gina woke me up at six-fifteen a.m. We had to be down at seven a.m. to catch the bus. Despite only having forty minutes of sleep, I wasn't tired. I just couldn't stop crying. I couldn't believe this was the end of my trip.

The bus driver started the bus and began to drive out of Lixouri. I couldn't see Alex, but I could feel him. I knew he was there. Looking out the bus window, I cried silently to myself.

Chapter 11

I t was official, I had arrived back home in Canada. Who would have ever thought I would find my soulmate on that trip? I certainly didn't. I thought I would have been lucky to see and enjoy some eye candy. I certainly wasn't expecting to meet and fall in love with the most incredible human being of all time.

That summer, I experienced thoughts, feelings and emotions I never thought were possible. The tiny village by the sea was an idyllic place to fall in love.

Next, I had to make it through ten months without him.

Albeit, was easier that everyone knew about him, including my parents. They seemed happy, which took a lot of stress off me. Going from not being allowed to talk to boys on the phone to them knowing and accepting I had a boyfriend was a big step. Granted, he did live across the world, so I think my dad thought it was pretty safe.

I received my first email from Alex a few days after being back in Canada. I was so happy, I cried. I missed him more than anything. The days and nights felt cold and lonely. It felt as though very little made me smile. How was I going to get through the long months ahead?

I began to make a cassette tape for him with some love songs on it and also with recordings of my voice. I knew it would drive him crazy, just as the sound of his voice did for me. I hand wrote him a letter and sealed it with a kiss. Bright red lipstick did the trick. I knew he would be beyond thrilled to receive a love package in the mail from me.

It was October nineteenth, the morning of my birthday. It didn't feel like a special day. In fact, it felt anything but. I just wanted to be with him.

When I returned home in the evening, there was a package for me on the kitchen table. I saw it was from him and quickly ripped it open. I stood there in amazement. There was the most beautiful red rose. It looked so fresh and alive. I couldn't believe it made its way from Greece to me without so much as a little wilt. I thought this was a powerful sign our relationship could withstand the test of time. He had also sent a cassette tape for me, a gorgeous outfit, a birthday card, and a few other things along with a handwritten letter. Receiving this package meant the world to me. His thoughtfulness and planning to get that gift to me on my exact birthday made me feel so loved and special.

Over the next eight months, we kept our promise of writing, calling and sending special packages to one another. We would also often send e-greeting cards to one another and it always put a smile on my face. It made the long days more bearable. We called the months of the calendar, 'pages' so that it seemed we would be together more quickly.

In March, we only had three pages to go. Thinking this way seemed to make living without him much more manageable.

Through the long days and nights without him, I cried myself to sleep more times than I care to remember.

After many nights of missing him, I decided that when we were together again, I would make love to him. Although I promised myself that I would remain a virgin until marriage, I had never experienced this connection with anyone before. Sex was sacred to me. It was something I felt should only be shared with your soulmate when you got married. In him, I knew I had found my forever. There was no reason to wait. I made the decision confidently. I knew eventually we would get married. I couldn't wait to share such a monumental experience with him.

Chapter 12

It had been the longest fall, winter and spring of my life. I could not wait to get back to Athena. I missed Alex so deeply. I spent every holiday, birthday and special moment wishing we were spending it together.

Needless to say, this summer, I went to Greece alone. To say I was chomping at the bit to get there would be an understatement. The lengthy time away from him made me realize the magnitude of which I loved and wanted to spend forever with him.

I searched high and low for the perfect piece of lingerie for our first night together. I wanted it to be white with silk and lace.

After months of searching, I found a piece that looked as sexy as it did elegant. Against my olive skin, it looked amazing. I felt so beautiful in it. Modeling it in my room in front of a mirror, I felt confident. I couldn't wait to see his reaction when I put it on for him. I knew he would light up.

I thought about our first night a million times over. I thought of every single detail. I was a little nervous but mostly very excited.

The flight to Athens was good, which is more than I could say for my nerves. I'm not sure why I was so nervous. I had an overabundance of butterflies in my stomach and my hands were clammy.

I took out my makeup bag as we began our descent into Athens. The long flight took any moisture I had in my skin and threw it out the window. I looked tired and dehydrated. Not exactly how I wanted to present myself to my Greek god waiting for me at the airport. Like the rose he sent me on my birthday, I wanted to look fresh and alive.

Other than a few photographs we had sent to each other via snail mail, we hadn't seen each other. I didn't forget what he looked like, I could never. However, it felt like I was seeing him again for the first time. I was a ball of nerves. I applied a few strokes of blush on each cheek and some translucent powder to lock everything in, and I was ready to go.

The summer heat of Athens hit me as I exited the aircraft. Walking down the long hallway, my legs felt like jelly. I tried hard to keep my composure but as I got closer to where he would be waiting for me, I felt a rush of excitement and nerves.

There he was, with a smile so big upon his face. Returning the giant smile, I ran into his arms. Every ounce of nerves I had quickly disappeared with the sight of his beautiful face and comforting embrace.

We hailed a taxi that would take us to his home. Sitting in the taxi, with excitement in his voice, he let me know his parents and sister had already left for the island. We had the house to ourselves for a week. For about a minute, I sat in shock. It was the greatest news ever. I felt like I had died and gone to heaven.

It would be the first time in our relationship we were able to have so much quality time, just him and I. No friends, no family, no passerby's and no three a.m. fishermen to contend with. No distractions, no time limit, nowhere to be but with each other. It felt like a dream that was too good to be true.

Sitting as close to each other as we could, our hands tightly intertwined, we couldn't stop looking and smiling at one another.

We needed to make a stop to pick up a part that had come in for his motorcycle. The taxi pulled in. It looked like a run-down hole in the wall. A stand-alone brick and mortar building surrounded by trees.

When we got out of the taxi, Alex advised the driver it was okay to leave. I had a puzzled look on my face which he caught and let me know we were within walking distance of his house. He asked me to stay back while he went to find someone who worked there.

While he was gone, a massive dog came to the deck baring his teeth and barking non-stop. His loud barking, big teeth and drool pouring down his face, had me scared shitless. I was sure he was going to eat me.

I began screaming for Alex as the dog came closer to me. The look of utter horror on my face was enough to spring Alex into action. He ran as quickly as he could and wrapped his body around mine. I was shaking, completely terrified. I hadn't noticed the dog was on a leash. He held me and told me I was safe.

It took a bit for my body to calm down after that traumatic incident. After it was all over with, we had a good laugh. It wasn't quite the first experience with him I had hoped for.

I breathed a huge sigh of relief as we arrived at his home. He gave me a tour and I marveled at how beautiful it was. His mother had a keen eye for design.

We ordered food in and enjoyed a flavorful candlelit dinner together. It was perfect. In the back of my mind, I knew I had that beautiful white babydoll outfit in my suitcase.

After dinner, I excused myself. I quickly grabbed the sexy lingerie from my suitcase and went into the washroom to put it on. I knew he would be shocked and I couldn't wait to see his reaction, but more than anything, I could not wait to feel his body close to mine again. It had been way too long.

I had decided to lose my virginity to him, but I hadn't told him yet. I wanted to be able to share my decision face to face. I knew it would be an incredible moment to experience together, in person.

I could hear him in the kitchen cleaning up the dishes. I went to his room and called for him to come. I felt so sexy wearing my lingerie. I stood with my hands up in the doorway, a pose straight out of a boudoir shoot.

When he saw me he dropped to his knees. He was speechless. I had goosebumps fill my body. He quickly got up and took me into his arms. We kissed so passionately. He laid me down on his bed. We were looking into each other's eyes and I said, "My love, I love you so much. We have waited such a long time for this moment together. I am ready. I want to make sweet, passionate love to you."

With tears in our eyes, our bodies pressed tighter together. He touched me with such care and gentleness. He had awoken all the parts of me that had been tucked away for so long. Feeling his magical fingers reveal my sweet juices felt indescribable.

I was more than ready. I wanted him inside of me more than anything, but first I wanted to reacquaint myself with his body. I wanted to smell, feel, taste and see every inch of him. I wanted to hear him moan as I rediscovered him.

The tingling sensations that ran through my body were a strong indication I was ready to receive him. I made my way on top of him, he guided his erection to the warmth between my legs. We looked deep into each other's eyes. It was powerful.

Slowly I began to take him inside of me. I could feel him throbbing as his hands held my hips. He helped to gently guide my body down his shaft. Together, we created slow and rhythmic movements as he thrust deeper inside of me.

Our bodies were shaking from the pleasure. It was as if we had merged into one. I felt like I was on fire in the best way. What in the hell was this magical feeling? Pleasure was pouring through my entire being.

We were completely lost in each other. Feeling his breath on my body, listening to our moans and watching him enjoy me made for faster and harder thrusting. Our orgasm was so close, we couldn't hold it. Feeling him and I orgasm at the same was the best feeling. I saw all the colours of the rainbow. It took some time for me to come out of what can only be described as a euphoric trance.

It goes without saying, my first experience was mind blowing. I was seeing multi-coloured stars and every part of my body was trembling. Although, to be honest, I expected nothing less. Our connection was out of this world. I was hooked. He was my drug and I needed more of where that came from.

I certainly didn't regret my decision. It felt right. We were our true, authentic selves with one another. It felt safe and comfortable. I knew I would never forget this experience for the rest of my life.

During our week of being alone together in Athens, we made love a lot. Like a whole lot.

But we also did other amazing things. I experienced what it felt like to ride as a passenger, through the streets of Athens on a motorcycle. What made driving in Athens most difficult for me as a foreigner, was the erratic driving of others. While Greek drivers are used to motorcycles squeezing between speeding cars, as they pass each other, I was not. I remember the first time Alex did this I was shocked. Pedestrians saturated the streets from all directions, I didn't think I'd make it out alive.

Alex took me to some of the most incredible cafés and restaurants in Athens. The views were spectacular. We made dinners together. I met some more of his friends and family. It was one of the best weeks of my entire life. I pinched myself a lot. I didn't know how I got so lucky.

Chapter 13

The trek to the island wasn't as long as I remembered it. Although, this time I experienced it with a whole new appreciation.

I loved being able to go on this adventure with him. Seeing the beautiful sights and sounds of Greece with someone I loved, made it feel like I was experiencing it for the first time.

We were two lovers immersed deeply in our affection for one another. We didn't need rose-colored glasses for everything to look beautiful, it just was. When we were together, the world was a better place.

His parents were waiting for us to arrive in Lixouri. They were ecstatic to see us. They welcomed us with open arms and big kisses, squealing as they hugged us. I felt like a celebrity. Being back together, feeling their love and being immersed in their happiness was restorative.

We went to his home first. His parents had cooked a delicious meal for us. They were excited to see me. Curious about who I was and how my life was back in Canada, they asked a lot of questions. I was happy to share as they listened intently with soft eyes and gleaming smiles. They seemed very happy we were together again.

That summer, Alex went back to his job as a waiter at the popular beach restaurant. It was the perfect job for him. He was great at what he did and he made good money doing it.

We spent a lot of time together before he went to work, after work, or both. He introduced me to more of his friends. One of whom I connected very well with. Her name was Elliana and she and her family lived in New York City. Her parents also have a summer home they come to every year.

They were the sweetest, kindest people. Their qualities trickled down through to their four children. Elliana and I laughed a lot together. Her sense of humour, love of life and caring heart made it easy to be around her. We both loved sports. She adored New York Yankee, Derek Jeter, while I could easily recite every stat on the Toronto Maple Leaf, Mats Sundin. She would often make fun of my Canadian accent and the fact I said 'eh' a lot. I teased her for saying 'huh' a ton.

Luckily, we got to spend a lot of time together. We would go to the beach together, watch the guys play soccer, go to the club, hang out at cafés and restaurants in Lixouri and I would go to her house to visit.

One time we decided to turn her house into a club. She even made a sign to put at the end of her long windy driveway that said Club Melenthro.

Their home was situated high on the hill making the view during the day or night spectacular. All of our friends and lots of Alex's family were there. Everyone was happy and enjoying the beautiful night. I remember taking a moment to sit out on her balcony. I looked at the moon, feeling the warmth of its glow touch deep inside of me. I closed my eyes and sat in gratitude. Gratitude for the moment, gratitude for my incredible partner, gratitude for amazing friends, gratitude for my health and gratitude for this amazing life.

I knew it wouldn't take long before I received a call saying my father was coming to Greece to meet Alex. I'm pretty sure it was blasphemous to my grandfather and uncles that I was allowed to have a boyfriend, especially so out in the open. Although, nothing was ever said to me. Truthfully, I didn't care. I wasn't rude or disrespectful, I just didn't want to put the pressure of hiding and secrecy on me or my relationship. I saw what my cousins and other girls in the village had to go through, and it wasn't me. Enduring a long-distance relationship was hard enough. After all, honesty is the best policy. Plus, I was an adult. I hoped my courage and bravery would help pave the way for others.

As it grew closer to his arrival, I felt nervous and excited to introduce him to Alex. I was sure he would love him, but I wasn't sure who was more nervous, me or Alex. My dad is a man of very few words. His heart is made of pure gold. He would do anything for anyone and expected nothing in return. I felt as though Alex and his parents were much the same. I knew the moment he met Alex and his family, he would understand why I was so smitten.

Of course, I was right. My dad approved of Alex and his family. They were sweet, kind and welcoming.

During my dad's stay, we shared a few dinners, great conversations and many laughs together. It was a huge step in our relationship. We had several talks of spending forever together.

The thought of moving to Greece felt realistic for me. I had always loved a challenge and Lord knows I was adventurous. If anyone could do it, it was me. I realized I would have to give up my dream of being a sports psychologist. Not because sports didn't exist in Greece, but because my Greek wasn't as strong as it should be for such a position. It was okay because what I would be getting instead would be a far greater reward to me. At the time, I didn't give it much more thought than that.

One of the things I loved was how caring and thoughtful Alex's parents were. When I visited his home, his dad would go out and pick fruit off the tree, clean it, cut it up and serve it to me. They always made sure I was doing okay and asked if there was anything I needed. I thought I had hit the parents-in-law jackpot.

The day had come when it was time to leave the beautiful island of Kefalonia once again. I knew it would be difficult, but this time, I was grateful Alex was able to come back to Athens with me.

It was an early morning, but the heat of the sun made it feel like the middle of the afternoon. We were down by the boat and needed to board. His parents and sister came to see us off. His mom couldn't stop hugging me and crying.

We made our way onto the boat. It was ready to leave and she couldn't let me go. Finally, people were yelling at her to get off the boat as it started to pull away from the dock. We had built a special connection with one another. She felt like a mother. It broke my heart to leave, and to see her so sad.

Alex and I soaked up all the alone time we had at his home in Athens. The longer we were together, the more difficult it was to say goodbye.

There were so many more experiences that summer with him. Most notably, the decision to lose my virginity to him. Experiencing something so intimate with a man who has fully captivated my heart, mind, body and soul was the greatest experience. How does one then get on a plane, and fly halfway around the world without him for another ten months?

The winter would be incredibly difficult, there were no two ways about it. But, it's just what we had to do. It was a sacrifice we were willing to make for one another. We knew we would make up for lost time when we saw one another again. We knew we wouldn't have to keep experiencing this dreadful parting for much longer. We had decided I was going to go back to Canada, finish school and move to Greece. There wasn't a question in our minds that we both wanted forever together.

Chapter 14

As soon as school started, I went into the guidance office to make an appointment with a guidance counsellor I had a great rapport with. I knew sports psychology wasn't an option if I wanted to live in Greece, so I needed a plan B.

I sat in Mr. Peets' office. He was quirky, fun, always happy and eager to help. We talked about my situation and without missing a beat, he looked at me with his piercing blue eyes and said, "You like beauty and helping people, why don't you look into cosmetology?"

Hmm. I hadn't considered that. He was right, I did appreciate all things beauty and I did really love to help people. He continued, "It's a career you can take anywhere in the world". He was absolutely right. How did I not think of this? He was on to something.

I left his office pretty excited. The search began. I would go on to spend hours researching different options and schools. I settled on an Esthetics program in a city an hour and a half away. I was able to complete the program fairly quickly in comparison to a four-year university degree.

Up until that point, the only experience I had with beauty in a spa setting was getting my eyebrows waxed. I had no idea what I would be getting myself into.

It was sometime in late September when my parents came to me with the idea of bringing Alex to our house for Christmas. I was ecstatic. I remember calling him immediately. He could hear the excitement in my voice and wondered what I was so excited about.

Through my squealing, I let him know my parents offered to bring him to Canada for Christmas. He was surprised and also very appreciative and grateful. I couldn't wait to show him where I lived, and places I liked to go, but most of all I couldn't wait to introduce him to my family and friends. I knew they would adore him as much as I did. After all, he was kind hearted, charming and easy on the eyes. What wasn't to love?

Every year, the Greek Community Banquet Hall puts on a New Years Eve dinner and dance. For years, I wanted to be a guest; however, I always had to work this event. This year, I bought two tickets. I didn't want to miss the opportunity, especially with my handsome Greek god.

I began searching for the perfect dress. I tried on many. Short, long, simple and over the top. I settled on a simple yet refined long mermaid style red dress with a black chiffon overlay. It had a seductive side slit that went more than halfway up my left leg.

We pulled into the arrivals area at Pearson International Airport in Toronto. I jumped out of the car and headed inside the airport while my parents parked.

By this point in my life, navigating an airport was second nature. I figured out pretty quickly where he would be coming off the plane.

The anticipation was killing me. I saw his flight had arrived. The butterflies and clammy hands returned, but I knew they wouldn't be there long. Everyone on his flight came out, except him. Did he miss the flight? Surely he would have called to let me know. This was very strange. Something didn't feel right. I knew he was on that flight. Where the hell was he? He couldn't have gotten lost, could he? I thought to myself.

An hour passed and still no sign of him. I was panicking. I asked anyone who looked like they could help, to help me.

Finally, over the loudspeaker, we heard my dad's name. They were paging him to Customs and Immigration. Customs and Immigration? What was going on?

We headed there as fast as we could hoping to get much needed answers. It felt like we had gone to jail. They wouldn't allow anyone in the secret room but my father.

Almost another hour went by. Finally, they both came out. I ran into his arms. He looked really happy to see me, but also like he'd been dragged through a knothole.

For no reason at all, they thought he was some sort of terrorist and they were giving him the third degree. My parents and I felt horrible for him. Needless to say, he didn't have a great start to his Canadian adventure. I hoped I could make it up to him.

It was a two-hour drive home from the airport. The first thing he noticed was all the snow on the ground. He'd never seen snow in real life. His eyes filled with wonder and excitement.

We stopped at an OnRoute on the way. The first thing he did when he got out of the vehicle was run to the snow and put his hands in it. He had the biggest smile on his face. His eyes were shining. We played around in the snow for a few minutes. My parents watched us with smiles on their faces. We grabbed a bite to eat and continued on our way home.

He seemed fascinated by our home. By living standards in Greece, we lived in a mansion. Our home was situated on a dead-end street out in the country with lots of trees on an acre lot. This was almost unheard of in Athens. It was peaceful. At night it was quiet and very dark. Much different from how he was used to living in Athens.

After dinner, it was dark outside but that didn't stop us from going out to make snowmen together. We were like two little kids getting to play outside in the snow.

First, we made the traditional snowman by rolling three balls of snow and placing them on top of one another. We even gave it a carrot nose, two eyes, a mouth, a hat and sticks for arms. My parents had a concrete pedestal table outside. We made a baby snowman with just one ball. It was the sweetest looking little snowman I ever saw. He loved it, and I loved seeing him so happy. We were freezing cold but had so much fun making snowmen, we laughed uncontrollably. That night I knew, you're never too old to rediscover life's magic again.

With each day that passed, he met more and more of my family and friends. As expected, they loved him. More importantly, they could see how much we loved one another. We were at the mall and the Santa village was set up. We stood in line to have our picture taken with jolly ol' St. Nick. Even Santa commented on how beautiful our love was.

Of course, we had to take Alex to see Niagara Falls. It was an iconic must-see for any new visitor to our part of the world. Being December and freezing cold, we didn't have to contend with the crazy amounts of tourists that normally flooded the area. We had unobstructed views wherever we went.

Going to Niagara Falls in the winter is one of the best times to visit because we were able to see the falls partially frozen. It was quite a sight to behold, surrounded by snow and ice. Our noses and cheeks were bright red as the chilling mist rose up above the falls and surrounded us. As far and wide as you could see, the glistening sparkle of snow and ice covered the trees, plants, railings and buildings alike. I felt fortunate to be able to experience this with him.

Waking up beside him on Christmas morning, seeing his smile and the softness of his eyes as he ran his fingers up and down my arm was the best gift ever. There was nothing I needed or wanted more than what I had at that moment.

To me, Christmas was the coziest time of the year. Spending time at home with the people we love the most, watching movies, surrounded by the heat of the woodstove, flickering of the lights and enjoying delicious foods and treats. It always brings warmth to my heart, and especially that year.

Being in a long-distance relationship really taught me the importance of mindfulness. I focused on the now and paid extra attention to the little things, knowing that moments together were precious. It was a funny thing though, it seemed to go out the window whenever we parted. I found in the long days and nights without him, I was never in the now. Most times, I wasn't even in the same month as the present.

I felt the black chiffon drape down my body as I put on my New Years Eve dress. My makeup and hair were perfectly done. I slid my feet into the sexy black Steve Madden heels I purchased specifically for this occassion.

He entered the room as I was taking one last glance in the mirror before heading downstairs. His eyes lit up. His arms opened wide. Held in his embrace he said. "Wow, you look incredibly beautiful, my love." Our eyes locked and we began to kiss. At first, it was soft, little pecks which turned into a fury of passionate kisses. I didn't want it to stop. I could feel he didn't either.

What a wonderful way to ring in the new year. We enjoyed a delicious Greek meal, amazing music, lots of dancing fast and slow, Greek and English. We listened to the crowd of people chant the countdown as we snuggled close to one another, sharing that famous New Year's kiss, as the clock struck midnight. We were moving into the promise of the new year with grateful hearts, excited for the many new adventures we would have together.

I hated to see him go. Aside from the hiccup at the airport, I think he loved Canada and the time we were able to spend together.

Chapter 15

This winter wasn't nearly as long as the winters past. We saw each other at Christmas, and I was finishing school early, so I decided to go to Greece in March. This meant missing my graduation and prom.

At the time, it wasn't a big deal because the reason I was going was far more important than walking across the stage. I wasn't willing to lose that much time with him just to get a piece of paper.

I kept my decision to go early a secret. I wanted to surprise him. I was like a kid at Christmas. I didn't know how I was going to keep this huge secret from him.

Upon my arrival in Athens, I went straight to my Theia Stamatoula's house. We devised a plan. She was going to call him and ask him to come to her house because I had sent packages in the mail for him.

Without question he said he was on his way. He lived less than twenty minutes from her house. In a city as big as Athens, I found it impressive he lived so close. Just like on the island, he lived in the next village, five minutes away. Well done, universe. Well done.

I had always been excited to see him after long periods of time apart, but this time was different. I was even more excited (if that was possible) because he didn't know I was there. I couldn't wait to see his reaction.

I paced around the house. My whole body was sweaty. I was giddy and nervous but mostly I was excited. The doorbell rang. My stomach dropped. I thought it was weird I didn't hear his motorcycle.

My Theia went to answer the door and I stood waiting by her couch. It was him. He came with his father in their car. When he saw me, he was motionless. It looked like he was lost. He could not speak. He looked at me as if he could not believe what he was seeing. He was definitely in shock.

Once the shock wore off we kissed and hugged. We were in front of my family and his father so we needed to be mindful. We couldn't stop looking at one another with huge smiles on our faces.

We stayed with my family for a little bit and then we went to his house. When we arrived, he and his dad stood back as I rang the doorbell.

His mom answered the door. When she saw me, she started screaming for joy. She was jumping up and down. She couldn't believe I was standing there. With all the commotion, his sister came running to the door. She reacted the same way. They hugged me tight as they led me into their home. It felt good to be so loved and accepted by his family.

I got to see him often over the four months we were in Athens together. Usually, he would pick me up on his motorcycle after school during the week, we would visit for a few hours and then he would bring me back to my Theia's house.

We had this thing where after he dropped me off late at night and had to drive his motorcycle back to his house, he would call my aunt's house when he arrived and let it ring once so that I knew he had made it home safely. It's the sweet little things that meant so much.

When we spent time at his place, we loved cuddling up on his bed to watch a movie, which mostly always ended in making love. I never complained. There was nothing on this earth I enjoyed more than making love to him. Truthfully, I couldn't get enough.

On the weekends we took rendezvous all over the city from the hot spots to some of the most incredible, off the beaten path hidden gems the city had to offer. It didn't matter what we did or didn't do, we were always immensely happy and grateful to be together.

On Saturday mornings his mom and I used to love going to outdoor flea markets together. The streets where the flea market took place became colourful and cheerful. We would mingle with locals and find anything our hearts desired. You could find the most eccentric and bizarre of items, and even a few treasures in between. Everything from gorgeous antiques to vintage jewelry, home goods, clothes and various other accessories. Sometimes his sister would come with us, but mostly it was our bonding time together and I looked forward to it.

My beautiful cousin Afroditi got married in Athens at the end of June. I had never been to a Greek wedding in Greece. I was happy to be there as she planned her big day. Excited to go to one of her dress fittings, I marveled at her. She looked stunning, much like a princess. Definitely, a goddess of beauty.

A Greek tradition I had no idea about was the 'making of the bed.' It is one of the most popular and well-known traditions in Greece. It took place before the wedding. Family and friends of my cousin and her soon-to-be husband gathered at their home to help with the preparation of the bed. The bed was bare and together we put the sheets and blanket on. Prosperity and putting down roots are symbolized by throwing money and rice onto the made bed, and then a baby is rolled on the bed to bless it with fertility. It was definitely neat to partake and learn about this fun tradition.

The wedding was a beautiful ceremony that took place in a stunning Greek church that boasted rich colours and distinctive iconography. The art and design of the church not only created a unique atmosphere of worship but also reflected and embodied many of the fundamental inspirations of Orthodoxy.

As a thank-you gift, the guests of the wedding were given beautifully packaged sugar-coated almonds after the ceremony. They symbolized purity, fertility, and the endurance of marriage.

After the ceremony, we headed to a quaint banquet hall to enjoy a night of great food, music and dancing. Being able to experience my first Greek wedding in Greece with my love was wonderful. I would be lying if I said I wasn't fantasizing about our own wedding.

After the wedding festivities were over, we were thrilled to be headed to Kefalonia. We both had enough of the bustle of Athens and really looked forward to the peace and serenity the island offered. We were also excited to see our friends and family.

It was much like summers before, we saw one another as often as we could. We spoke a lot about our future. We both wanted to get married and have lots of children. I felt as ready as one could ever feel. If he had proposed that summer, it would have been a resounding YES! When you know, you know. There wasn't a chance I would ever feel this magic with anyone else. It was truly too good for words.

At the end of July, we celebrated our third anniversary. He was meticulous in his desire to make me feel special. When he arrived, his hair was perfectly styled, his facial hair flawlessly trimmed and his attire made him look remarkably sexy. He handed me a dozen beautiful red roses arranged in a bouquet with greenery and baby's breath. I took a moment to breathe in their sweet aroma.

For dinner, we drove to a distinguished restaurant with fancy table linens and servers who wore black bow ties, black vests, and crisp white shirts. Our dining experience included an incredible view of the water, mountains and an abundance of tiny twinkling lights. Romance filled the air.

After dinner, hand in hand, we went for a romantic walk around the city. Strolling, we reminisced about the many memories we had made together over the years. We laughed a lot, sharing story after story. Goosebumps filled my body with just the touch of his hand and the unspoken word of his love and adoration for me.

He surprised me with a night at a luxurious hotel. He lit candles that provided a soft flickering light. We slid into each other's arms as our hips began to move in tandem. I took pleasure in the scent of his body and the way he could so powerfully and confidently hold me close to him. He took the lead as we slowly danced around the room. I moved back slightly and began unbuttoning his dress shirt. I traced my fingertips through the hair on his chest, looking into his eyes. I burned with desire. You can imagine how the rest of the evening transpired. I felt beyond fortunate to have had this incredible man in my life for three years thus far.

This was the summer many celebrities visited Kefalonia, Madonna and Tom Cruise to name a few. It was all over the Greek news. Nicolas Cage and Penelope Cruz were filming Captain Corelli's Mandolin in the village of Sami, which was about an hour drive from where we were located.

Sami has a charming waterfront, boasting wide paved streets with Venetian buildings that lined the streets. Famous for their underground caves including the particularly famous Melissani Cave. It is the most startlingly beautiful geological phenomenon. It was discovered in 1951 after a cave collapsed, revealing a gorgeous lagoon below.

On one of our trips to Sami, Alex and I visited Melissani. I found it fascinating, being in a small boat inside that caved lagoon seeing how the sun reflected down illuminating the water. Viewing the different rock formations and the indescribable colours was a sight to be seen.

We took many day trips to Sami to see if we could catch a glimpse of the Hollywood stars. We never did, but it was exciting to have our little island put on the map.

After searching around Sami for a bit, we would find a new little café we hadn't been to before to enjoy lunch or dinner. I really treasured our alone time together. With him, I felt alive and seen.

It was so easy and comfortable for us to be sitting at a table just looking into each other's eyes without needing to speak any words. We were so energetically aligned. It was never awkward, never uncomfortable or weird. In fact, the magic we created by the simple act of eye gazing was pretty phenomenal. The world around us disappeared. Not to mention the increased sexual arousal it stirred up.

Things began to take a bit of a noticeable turn with his mother sometime in August. Since I was able to be in Greece for more than a summer, I discovered this dream of living there was not realistic. Don't get me wrong, it is a stunningly beautiful country and the food is so fresh and delicious but living in Greece wasn't easy. It wasn't the way I was used to living in Canada.

So many things were different - the currency, the language, technology, the economy, the health care system, and the development of civilization. They seemed to be so far behind in everything. Even Young and the Restless was seven years behind.

Oh, and they didn't have hockey! The Ontario Hockey League (OHL) and the National Hockey League (NHL) were my life back home. I couldn't imagine not being able to head out for a game whenever I wanted. Furthermore, I couldn't imagine not being able to take my future kids to games or take them to their own hockey practices and games. I thought about my kids going to school in Greece and how helpless I would feel not being able to help them with their homework or be able to participate in the school council. Would I even be able to fully understand their school plays?

I began to have so many questions about our future, and it made me worry. I was especially concerned about missing my family and friends. Sure, eventually I would adjust to living in Greece, but I feared it would take a toll on my happiness and eventually our relationship.

I knew in my heart of hearts, I couldn't live in Greece. Now I understood why Katerina was in tears that day on the ferry to Argostoli. I thought the solution was pretty easy. He would move to Canada. I knew we would have a better life in Canada. In hindsight, I was being pretty selfish. I wanted the proverbial cake and I wanted to eat it too.

I began to tell him my feelings. And after many conversations about this, he agreed with me and said he would move to Canada. Without a second thought, I was ecstatic.

What happened next would change everything! I was excited and consequently began to tell everyone that Alex was going to move to Canada. I did so with such enthusiasm and sparkle in my eyes. Nothing about my approach was humble or reserved. I could see our beautiful future so clearly. I could envision our life in Canada being happy, full of fun adventures and many awesome first-time experiences for him, like the magic of his first snow experience. Our children would grow up in a home full of so much love and happiness. They would live a life full of opportunities. They would see how much love their parents had for each other every single day. I could see it all.

It was late August. He had been working long, exhausting hours in the heat of the summer. I could see it was taking a toll on his body. He needed some rejuvenation and we were craving some quality time together. The thought of getting to spend a few days and nights with him alone had me over the moon. It had been far too long since we had that much time, just the two of us.

Arriving at my village early in the morning, I heard the low roar of his motorcycle. As he got closer, he turned it off and let it coast. He was respectful of others. He did this when it was late at night too. It was another quality of his that I found very attractive.

His bright eyes and smile when he saw me was enough to heat the crisp, cool morning air.

He got off his motorcycle to greet me. He looked sexy as always. Pulling me in close to him, we kissed an extra-long kiss good morning. I felt goosebumps all over my body. As he cradled me in his arms, looking into my eyes he told me he loved me. Kissing him once more, with a twinkle in my eyes, I told him I loved him too. We were both excited and ready for what the weekend would bring us.

I saddled in nice and close. My arms wrapped around his waist and my head rested on his shoulder close to his neck. We made our way into Lixouri for a quick bite to eat before heading off on our little adventure.

Alex and I decided we would take a trip to Ithaki for a few days to escape everything happening on the island. We stayed at the most adorable little studio. We spent time touring around the mountainous island, enjoying peaceful walks and calm swimming in emerald waters. We also spent a lot of time in bed together. Soaking up each other before I had to leave again. It was gut wrenching to think about. We needed this alone time, now more than ever.

My intuition was strong. I could count on it in any and every situation, especially when it came to people I loved.

I could feel something was off with his family, however, he assured me everything was okay.

On our way back to Kefalonia on his motorcycle, we had overpacked and it was pouring rain. Just as we made a turn to go around a bend, the front wheel lost grip. The motorcycle quickly flipped, and we were thrown off to the right side. It happened so fast. He got up and ran toward me to make sure I was ok. I was in shock. We both were.

We sat on the side of the road in the pouring rain, bleeding, holding one another. Once the shock wore off, I began to cry. He held me close and made me laugh as only he could. He kissed my forehead and told me he loved me. With that, we were back on the motorcycle, which thankfully wasn't too badly damaged. We had no medical supplies with us at all. We drove twenty minutes to the nearest pharmacy to get patched up.

It had been a very long morning. By the time we got back to his parents' home in the village, it was late afternoon. When we arrived, he told his mother what happened. She saw the damage on his body and shrieked. She hugged him tightly but did not even look at me. My heart sank. This was definitely not the reaction I expected based on our history together. Something was definitely wrong.

During our little getaway, we collected some colorful rocks that were in unique shapes and sizes. We sat at the kitchen table shellacking them. I tried to make her laugh, only to be met with coldness. Being a sensitive and empathetic soul, this caused a real stir inside my body. I was days away from going back to Canada and I couldn't bear the thought of leaving under these circumstances.

Unfortunately, once his parents found out what our plan was, of their son moving to Canada, they didn't feel the same toward me. The love and adoration they had for me disappeared very quickly. Understandably, they loved their son beyond measure. They would be damned if I took him to the other side of the world to live.

His mother, father and sister no longer had a gleaming smile from ear to ear on their faces when they saw me. Instead, they seemed cold and uninviting despite my efforts. I was beyond devastated.

For the last few nights on the island, we made our rounds to our family and friends to say our goodbyes. We had made many incredible memories together this summer.

His father brought us to Lixouri early in the morning the day we left the island. He said goodbye to me but it wasn't the same. It was weird and awkward. His mother didn't come, nor did she say goodbye. I felt so sad leaving the island. It wasn't at all like anything I had experienced in previous years. It didn't feel good. He tried to reassure me everything was ok. I knew he so desperately wanted it to be. But it wasn't.

We had just a few days together in Athens before my flight home. We needed this time to focus on each other.

Chapter 16

September 11, 2001

Goodbyes were never easy. In fact, they were dreadful. Being in a long-distance relationship meant the goodbyes were always looming in the back of our minds. We tried not to think about it as we made an effort to enjoy every day to its fullest. However, each day that passed was one day closer to one of us staying and one of us walking away.

From the moment we arrived at the airport there was a pit in my stomach. I gripped his hand tightly as we walked together through the airport. It didn't feel as though time was on our side. It felt like it was going at lightning speed. Before I knew it, there we were standing at the gate. Tightly embraced.

He remained calm and strong. So supportive and attentive to me. His kisses continued to feel warm and loving, making every final second harder than the last.

In tears, we pried ourselves apart knowing that if we didn't, I would miss my flight. It was the absolute hardest goodbye.

Leaving him at that gate in that airport was one of the hardest things I had ever done. My body felt weak, it was hard to breathe and I felt like I had cried a river. There were people everywhere hustling and bustling yet, I had never felt more alone.

Leaving him was beyond difficult just like many times before, but this time was different. Deep down I knew something was off. I didn't know what our future held or where our relationship was headed.

Looking out the tiny plane window, I wept. The plane sat on the tarmac for what felt like hours. I was getting impatient. All passengers had boarded and there we sat. And sat. And sat. It seemed like a cruel joke. Or, was it a huge sign from the universe to get off the plane and run as fast as I could back into his arms?

The P.A system bell rang, and I knew an announcement was coming. Finally. "This is your Captain speaking. We're sorry for the delay. There is luggage on the aircraft which needs to be taken off. We are working as quickly as we can to get this resolved. Thank you for your understanding".

Well, this was a first for me. In all the years I had flown, I had never experienced a delay because luggage needed to be taken off the aircraft. I didn't put too much brainpower into it. I honestly didn't have any to give. It was what it was and there was nothing I could do to change it. So I returned to my thoughts and waited patiently like everyone else.

Finally, I felt the aircraft begin to move. As the flight started to ascend, my heart began to tear even more.

About seven hours into the excruciatingly long flight, I was watching the moving-map system. This was a real-time flight information video broadcast through the screen in front of me. It displayed a map that illustrated the position and direction of the plane, the altitude, airspeed, outside air temperature, distance to the destination, distance from the origination point, and origin/destination/local time (using both the 12-hour and 24-hour clocks). The moving-map system information is derived in real-time from the aircraft's flight computer systems.

I noticed our destination kept changing. I'd never experienced that before either. It bounced around between Montreal, Halifax and Newfoundland. I was running on no sleep, barely on any food and a broken heart but I knew for certain I was on the right plane which was supposed to be headed to Toronto.

I wasn't the only one who noticed our end destination was not Toronto. I began to hear rumblings of terrorist attacks. My body went numb. People started to panic. The noise level on the plane went from a low hush to not being able to hear myself think.

A middle-aged lady was sitting beside me who looked just like Marlena from Days of our Lives. It was fitting because quite honestly, after everything I was hearing I felt like I might be living the last day of my life. She offered me her credit card so I could use the phone to call my parents.

"Hi, Mom and Dad, it's me, Effie," I began as my voice trembled. I tried to keep it together. I didn't want to scare or worry them. "I'm on the plane and I am okay. I don't know what's going on. I think we are being diverted but I'm not sure where. If something happens and I don't make it, please know I love you very much. Tell Vi and Jerry I love them, too. Okay, I have to go. I will call you as soon as I can. I love you, bye." I gripped the phone tighter as I pushed my ear into the receiver. I wanted so badly to feel closer to them. I needed them.

My parents were getting ready to pick me up from Pearson International Airport in Toronto. They of course knew what was happening that morning. They were told our flight was being diverted to Montreal so they began to drive to Montreal. An hour into their drive they were told the flight I was on was not being diverted to Montreal but to Halifax instead.

The next few hours were intense. Between plane turbulence, the uncertainty of what was happening, and being alone all I could do was sit in numbness. I could feel my heart racing.

With each jerk of the plane, I clutched the seat harder. Any turbulence at all made my blood pressure skyrocket and my heart pound. I could hear the noise but felt like I was in a tunnel. I closed my eyes and started to focus on my breath. That was something I could control and at that moment I needed to feel in control of something.

I felt the wheels hit the runway, and a chill ran over my body as I let out a huge sigh of relief. The plane erupted in clapping and cheers. Needless to say, we were all feeling pretty grateful.

After six hours of sitting on the tarmac and being on the aircraft for a total of nineteen hours, we were finally allowed to disembark. The airport was a lot smaller than I had expected yet the mass amount of people seemed strange.

The first thing I noticed were the phone banks that were set up. Airport staff were encouraging people to call their loved ones. The first number I called was, of course, Alex's. His father answered but wasn't his usual happy self when he heard my voice. He told me Alex wasn't there and didn't know when he would return. I called back a few more times with no luck. My heart sank.

I was still not sure what was going on or where we were going. I was flying with Olympic Airways. We were put on a bus which took us to a nearby Greek church.

When we arrived at the church there was an abundance of food, clothing and toys to make sure all passengers on the flight were taken care of. It was an incredible show of solidarity. The Greek community came through for us in a big way.

A TV was on at the back of the church hall where most people were gathered. This is where we found out and saw exactly what was happening and why we were in Halifax. Because of the volume of flights that needed to be diverted that catastrophic day, Halifax was the first international airport, with road and rail transportation to the rest of Canada, that was able to serve us.

Watching the news of the attacks that had taken place that fateful morning was shocking, to say the least. It was hard to believe. Families and friends huddled together watching the devastation as it was being reported. Jaws were agape and eyes were filled with tears. The room was filled with utter shock and disbelief.

I must have looked quite distraught. I remember pacing around before finally sitting in a chair. Elliana! Her name screamed into my thoughts. My heart was palpitating, I needed to know, was she ok? What about her family? Now, an even bigger lump in my throat and a pit in my stomach. The worst part was, I wasn't able to find out right away. I had to wait until I got home to call her.

I was sad, alone and scared. I had no idea how long I would be there or when I would be able to see my family. I wanted so badly to speak with Alex. I needed him to know I was okay. I knew he would be worried sick.

As the night came to an end and people were starting to wind down and get ready to try to go to sleep, a young lady came up to me and introduced herself. Her name was as beautiful as she was.

Anastacia asked if I wanted to come to her house to stay until we were allowed to fly out. I was a bit taken aback and not sure but I knew I didn't want to stay alone in the church. She didn't seem to be much older than me. I had been watching her as she was tirelessly helping out all night. Not only had she offered me a warm place to stay, but she also took in another couple who had a tiny baby and another couple with a pre-teen daughter.

I distinctly remember getting to her home. To me, she lived in a castle! The most stunning home and property I'd ever seen. As it turns out she was a writer and her husband was a doctor. They had two children of their own. Their living room looked like something out of a magazine, complete with a grand piano.

That night I remember she gave me her daughter's bedroom to stay in. I remember her little girl showing me around her room. Surprisingly, she was happy I was going to be taking over her space. Her bed was like something out of the movies. It was a queen-size bed that stood 4 feet off the ground. You needed a ladder to get up into it.

As my head hit the pillow, I discovered it was the absolute most comfortable bed I had ever been in. I cried. I actually sobbed. I felt so incredibly grateful to be alive and how fortunate I was to be in the care of such wonderful people.

The next morning, I was able to email Alex. I missed him so much. I would have given anything to be in his warm, strong, loving embrace. I wanted to find comfort in his eyes and the way they made me melt.

While I was composing my email, the young girl, Despina who was taken in along with her parents asked me if I would help her set up her first email address. I remember how excited I was to get my first email so I was thrilled to be able to help her get hers!

I remember Anastacia taught us the importance of washing fruits and vegetables. She was passionate about food. She took pride in her cooking and it showed. It was simple, yet pleasingly delicious. For breakfast or lunch, I recall eating many toasted tomato and mayo sandwiches as she knew it was a meal I loved. She truly was an earth angel who made us feel so loved and cared for.

Over the next five days, that amazing lady toured all of us around Halifax. Getting to go to the waterfront boardwalk in Halifax was so beautiful. We stopped to take a picture of us all together.

We went for walks daily around their gorgeous property and around the quiet streets where they lived. We watched movies at night with their family. I couldn't have been luckier to be in the care of these amazing souls. They graciously opened their home and their hearts to strangers and it still has me in awe.

After five days of this unexpected detour, our time in Halifax came to an end. Anastacia drove us to the airport. I was admiring the beauty of Halifax and feeling so grateful for her love and kindness. It helped to restore my faith in humanity after everything that transpired that fateful September morning.

At the airport, I was ready to fly back to Toronto on our original plane, when we had another delay. This time it was because there was a tonne of figs that were forgotten in the belly of the aircraft and they had rotted. It was a disgusting, horrible smell. Needless to say, they were trying to air out the plane.

Getting on that flight sure as hell required me to dig deep. I had to go back to that carefree little seven-year-old girl who boarded a flight to go across the world for an entire summer by herself. I needed her. I needed her bravery and her innocence. Right then I needed to embody the safety she felt as she admired the pearly white smiles of the flight attendants. I needed to trust everything was going to be okay. At this point in my life, being on an airplane was almost like second nature. Yet, for the first time, I was terrified. My body sat in the seat and trembled.

Smell and all, we were finally in the air headed to Toronto. The flight was quiet. You could feel everyone's exhaustion. Luckily, it wasn't a long flight. I was happy to be reunited with my parents, but it was bittersweet. I was an emotional mess. How would I even begin to process everything I had been through?

Chapter 17

I didn't arrive home until September sixteenth and I was supposed to start post-secondary education on September seventeenth. The school was almost two hours away from home. It was a mad rush to find a place to live, get settled and start learning this trade I was supposed to practice abroad. It was a whirlwind.

My hand picked up the telephone and my fingers began to dial her number. I was incredibly nervous. I had to make a conscious effort to not squeeze the receiver into my ear. Her mother answered and I felt a wave of relief. She was appreciative to receive a call from me and passed the phone to her eldest daughter, Elliana.

Our conversation focused mostly on the tragedy that took place in her beloved home of NYC. Hearing her smile through the phone made my heart happy. I understood many weren't so fortunate. We shared a meaningful conversation and I was eternally grateful she and her family were safe.

My mind kept busy as I got ready to move out of my childhood home. I found a room for rent in the basement of a townhouse. It certainly wasn't anything fancy, far from it, but it kept me warm, dry and safe.

I spent a few days settling into my new living space and school. Back then, I didn't have a cell phone and social media didn't exist. I had an email address and a landline telephone. It's hard to remember back to a time when we weren't so accessible. It would have been nice to have the technology to FaceTime or to instant message, especially with the time difference. Not spending thousands of dollars on phone bills would have also been pretty great. However, looking back, it made the communication we did have extra special.

I had the opportunity to speak to Alex a few times since being home. If there was anything that could calm, ground, soothe and excite me it was the sound of his voice. Everything seemed great, until I received a phone call that turned my world upside down.

It was seven p.m. my time, therefore it was two a.m. in Greece. Alex didn't usually call me so late. I was excited to speak with him nonetheless.

In his broken English, "Effie," he began, "I will tell you something right now and I really want you to understand. We cannot continue." My heart shattered.

"I want you to understand what I am saying and continue your life without me. It is hard for me, too. Maybe you don't believe me but that is how it is. I will not say many things. I want you to forgive me because I know I really hurt you right now. I want you to know I am hurting too. We just cannot continue. I can't love you anymore."

Through my gasps and wailing, he continued. "Please, it's for our own good, mostly for you. I know you will destroy your life here. I don't want that. Be strong and I will do the same. I wish the God who is up there will take care of you.

I will be praying every night for you." By this time, I felt like I was hyperventilating. I had never felt pain so deeply. The words he spoke were absolutely awful.

We were supposed to get married, have babies and live a beautiful life together. Nothing on this earth made me happier than how I felt when I was with him. Life felt so colourful and bright with him by my side. I wasn't prepared for that to be taken away. Not now, not ever.

As I sat there, I was trying to process what took place days before all the while trying to also grieve the loss of this incredible man and our relationship.

Tears streamed down my face. I felt so broken, unable to make sense of any of it. Thousands and thousands were grieving the loss of life. The death of their husband, wife, mother, father, brother, sister, son, daughter, aunt, uncle, cousin and friend. Our nation was grieving this horrendous, unthinkable tragedy - how could I possibly allow myself to feel the pain of losing the love of my life when so many others were suffering much, much worse? My heart hurt so badly for them, for the unfathomable heartache they were having to endure. But I was hurting too, and I needed to honour that.

I had a dream of becoming a sports psychologist. Instead, I chose a career where I could study and graduate in a fairly timely manner so that I could move to Greece as quickly as possible. I envisioned owning a successful two-storey spa where couples would come to retreat together in Athens. Of course, my parents wanted me to follow my dreams of becoming a sports psychologist. Though, I assured them that following my heart was equally as important.

In the days that followed the devastating phone call from Alex, I was distraught. I felt like a shell of the person I once was. I didn't know how to continue on without him. Getting out of bed every day took a lot of strength. The bags and dark circles under my eyes were an easy tell of the pain I was feeling.

To make matters worse, a week after the call I received from Alex, my parents received a letter in the mail from his parents in Greece. In the letter, they asked my parents to keep me (their daughter) away from him (their son) and in turn, they would keep their son away from me. I never in a million years thought I would be at the centre of a modern-day Romeo and Juliet story.

At the time I didn't understand why the sudden change, from one extreme to the other. How could they go from loving and adoring me so much to causing me an immense amount of hurt and pain? Didn't they want to see their son happy? How could they deny their son this incredible love? How could they do this to him and to us?

Now I understand it. So clearly. For the longest time, I carried around so much hurt. However, I felt a change when I had my first child. A beautiful baby boy.

When you're a mother, your brain changes. You think differently. I felt like my whole being was on this planet to love and care for this sweet child of mine. I could not begin to imagine if someone came to Canada from Greece, met either one of my boys, fell madly in love and said they were going to take him back to Greece. They would be on the fastest flight out of here. I'm kidding, of course. But honestly, it would be a hard pill to swallow.

So to be fair, I cannot blame his parents one bit. It took understanding, growth and experience for me to get to a place where I could let it go. I healed and became stronger and more aware because of it.

Chapter 18

I would spend the next year calling him as often as I could. It was mentally and emotionally difficult for both of us. I wasn't ready to let him go. I couldn't see a future without him in it. For three years we shared an incredible experience and a bond like none other. We were so wildly connected, and to have it gone? I couldn't comprehend it.

At the time I didn't have the resources or tools to help me navigate through this heartbreak. My heart, mind, body and soul could not come to terms with this relationship ending. In those rawest moments, I lost control of myself and my emotions. The pain was too much.

Calling and emailing him constantly left me feeling like a lunatic at times. My actions were irrational. I pushed him further away. His words became hurtful. "I love you" turned into "please stop calling me" and "just leave me alone." He wasn't the same person I had fallen so madly in love with. Yet, I persisted.

A little over a year later, in November of 2002, I was able to convince him to see me again. I flew back to Greece for a week. I needed to see him. I was hoping once he saw me, he wouldn't be able to let me go. I figured it was a lot easier to hide his feelings over the phone and through email. But could he look me in the eyes and tell me he didn't love me? He couldn't. That's the truth. He knew it and I knew it.

I had butterflies in my stomach waiting for him to arrive at my family's home in Peristeri. The anticipation of seeing him and the unknown of what would transpire had my stomach in knots. I felt sick.

I heard his motorcycle before he had a chance to knock on the door. I took a second to gather myself and then ran to the door. I flung the door open and there I stood wide-eyed, much like a deer caught in headlights. With a huge smile on my face, our eyes connected. I saw his smile and the gleam in his eyes and tears began streaming down my face. They were tears of joy. I had never been so happy to see anyone in my entire life. The feeling was mutual.

I ran into his arms and wrapped my legs around his body. He held me in his arms so tightly. Our lips connected and danced as beautifully together as they had all the times before. It was as if no time had passed. I felt the weight of the world lifted off my shoulders. It felt like the immense heartache and pain I had experienced over the last year had vanished. Seeing him and being in his arms, I felt like I was home.

I saddled into the back of his motorcycle and immediately wrapped my arms tightly around him. I relished the scent of him. His pheromones made my body squirm in pleasure. My lips were like a magnet to his neck, I couldn't help but give him little kisses as we headed off into the night.

I had no idea where we were going. He wanted to take me somewhere and that was good enough for me. I thoroughly enjoyed every second of being nestled so close to his body.

When we arrived, the sign on the building read *XXX Hotel*. I was puzzled. Where were we? He clasped my hand and we headed toward the door.

From the lobby, it seemed like a beautiful hotel. The front desk associate handed Alex a binder. Inside the binder were photos of different exotic-themed rooms. I was taken aback. Not in a bad way, but it wasn't something I was expecting.

It was perfect actually. There was nowhere else in the world I would rather be than in a hotel with the love of my life after the last year apart. He could have chosen a room with a monkey swinging from the ceiling and I would have been more than happy. Walking to the room hand in hand, I couldn't believe we were there. Together.

Dry ice filled the room as we walked in. Mirrors were hung wall to wall and a huge red heart-shaped bed with a canopy sprawled in the middle of the room.

He pinned me against the wall. His chin dropped, revealing the sharp features of his jawline in the shadow. His eyes slowly lifted and fixed on me as his hands hugged my face.

After a few seconds of looking right into each other's eyes, feeling his breath on my face he said "Did you really think I ever stopped loving you?"

My heart was pounding as tears filled my eyes. This was the moment I had been waiting for. Nothing could have made me happier. I felt weak in the knees. Our lips locked. How I missed the sweetness of his lips on mine. Our kisses were full of desire and passion. Like I remembered. Our bodies pressed firmly together.

His walls came tumbling down as we stood there fully embraced, passionately kissing. Under my blue silk blouse, I could feel my nipples were hard. I was aching, throbbing for his touch.

Undressing as quickly as we could, I needed and wanted to feel my body on top of his. I had been craving him for far too long and now it was time to unleash that desire.

With his strong arms, he lifted me onto the bed. Delicately securing me down with his hands around my forearms. I felt his warm breath on my neck. I had goosebumps over my entire body. In my ear he whispered, "I love you, Efoula mou." I melted.

Slowly and passionately, we indulged in each other. We felt the undeniable magic of making love to one another once again. Making love to him was always phenomenal but tonight proved to be the most euphoric experience yet. I felt whole again.

The next night he picked me up in his silver Audi. It was strange to be in a moving vehicle and not to be snuggled behind him. At the same time, we were able to maintain great conversation. We drove past his family home and I felt a bit guilty. If his parents knew I was in the country, in a car with their son, driving past their home, I'm not sure what their reaction would be.

Alex and I agreed we were going to do whatever it took to make our relationship work. Neither one of us had been this happy in over a year. I couldn't stop smiling the whole car ride.

We held hands, made each other laugh, and had some interesting chats. In quiet moments we listened to Greek music on the radio as he drove through the dark streets of Athens. My favourite song, Ax Koritsi mou by my all-time favourite Greek singer, Giannis Ploutarhos came on the radio. We both looked at each other and smiled. It gave me full body goosebumps.

Ax Koritsi mou is a love song which means, Oh my girl. The song is about a man who is deeply in love with a woman. He has waited so long for her to secretly arrive to look into his eyes. He would do anything for her. His soul is for her and no one else. He doesn't want her to go. The song is quite tender and romantic. The words perfectly echo the feelings we have for each other. It couldn't have played at a more perfect time. Oh, Universe. I thought as a quiet smile appeared on my face. I felt him grip my hand a little tighter. My heart skipped a beat.

Alex took me to see his cousin, Cassie. I was shocked but I guess he was excited to share the news of my arrival and our reconciliation. I felt as though this was a major act on his part solidifying his commitment to me, to us. His family is a close-knit unit and would surely hear the news quickly. Cassie, along with his other cousin, Thalia, were my favourites. It was lovely to see her again. I enjoyed spending time with her. Yet, we didn't stay long.

What happened next would be the final straw.

The last night I was in Athens before coming home to Canada, Alex came to see me. I hated to leave him again. But we had made a plan. It wasn't as difficult to leave knowing we were going to work hard to make our relationship last. We were going to drown out all the outside voices and just listen to our hearts.

He arrived with a different look in his eyes. I immediately knew it was the end. My face felt hot. I felt a pain in my chest and tears began to fill my big brown eyes as we stood on the sidewalk just outside my Theia's house.

The trees that lined the street swayed peacefully in the breeze. We hugged tighter than ever before, knowing this would be the last one. Tears poured down my makeup-filled face. He cried as he swept my hair behind my ear.

After moments of silence, he started to speak. I carefully listened as he told me we couldn't continue our relationship. It was too difficult for him. He could never move to Canada and he could never allow me to leave my life in Canada for him. He knew I wouldn't be completely happy living in Greece. He was trying to be so strong but I knew he was dying inside.

It was a chilly night. I sobbed in his arms and my body shook. My chest hurt as I struggled to breathe. The bright stars glistened in the sky. They were the same stars we had made love under many, many times before.

We would kiss one final time. His silky, warm lips felt too good to stop. Black mascara lined my cheeks continuing down my neck. I looked like something out of a horror show.

I watched as he mounted his motorcycle. My body was weak. I wished there was something more I could say or do.

He blew me a kiss and off he went. It felt like a knife was ripping my heart into millions of tiny pieces. I stood outside until I couldn't hear the sound of his motorcycle anymore. Perhaps even a little longer in case he chose to come back. He didn't.

As I lay in bed, feeling numb, I heard one last final ring of the telephone when he arrived home. I knew he made it safely and that was it.

It was on this trip my eyes opened to the fact he didn't build walls to keep me out. He did so out of necessity to protect whatever he had left within. This realization didn't make the face-to-face break-up easier by any means. We were both broken and hurt. It wasn't fair for me to take any more than he had to give. I needed to protect whatever he had left. I loved him enough to at least give him that. He had been trying to do that for me.

Do I regret going back to see him? No. It was pivotal in helping me understand and begin to heal. The love we shared for one another was like none other. But we weren't meant to stay together as one. The universe had other plans for us. We needed to trust and look at the bigger picture, even though that was much easier said than done.

Chapter 19

A t times, the thought of being open and vulnerable enough to find love again seemed like something I was neither mentally or emotionally capable of doing. I honestly could not fathom the idea.

However, as time went on the fibres of my broken heart slowly began to mend. I didn't want my experience of such significant heartbreak to prevent me from opening my heart again to the possibility of love. I understood how powerful love could be and how incredible it felt. I knew I couldn't deny myself the opportunity to experience true love again.

I also knew that to find "the one," I needed to find and love myself. I admit I was a broken mess. Where and how would I even begin to heal?

At first, it was by taking it one minute at a time. I permitted myself to grieve and to feel every emotion I needed to feel in those moments. Most days I would fall to my knees, screaming and crying. It was messy and the pain was crippling.

Our internal compass is the navigational system that guides our emotional, spiritual and mental direction. When we are brave and open enough to intuitively listen, this significant tool is both vital and effective in steering us through our darkest days.

It takes time, but healing is possible. Coming out on the other side of pain was a beautiful journey of self-awareness and self-discovery for me.

Over time and through life experiences, I came to understand that the end of our relationship was ultimately in my (our) best interest. I have since acknowledged what a stepping stone our relationship was on my path and how it would prepare me for what was to come.

Throughout the years, after multiple boyfriends and random hookups, I'd given up on the idea of finding my soulmate again. I was fed up with the process of finding love. I was tired of meeting and dating people who weren't the right match for me. I felt like I had exhausted all options, from in-person to online. I had come to terms with having found and lost my one true soulmate in this lifetime. Who was I to believe that I deserved this once-in-a-lifetime person twice?

In 2008, after many years of hurt and pain, I was blessed to meet my wonderful husband. The way we met was serendipitous. I knew he was someone special when I felt that magical spark, the one I felt ten years before.

It was more than being in the right place at the right time. I knew the universe was working behind the scenes to make this forever connection happen.

What I've learned is that love enters your life when you least expect it. It's ironic, but detaching myself from the idea of attracting my soulmate was the key to getting what I wanted faster. When I truly surrendered and got out of my own way, I released the barriers that held me back.

This was when the universe responded. As I let go of expectations, embraced vulnerability and gave way to the universe, that's when the magic happened. This is when he was put in my path to renew my faith in divine timing.

Meeting and falling in love with him has been an extraordinary experience. One I wouldn't have been able to believe was possible. Not only is he a remarkable husband who puts me and our family before everything else, but he is also an incredible father to our two beautiful children, Nikolas and Lukas. I am so fortunate to have found and experienced true love twice.

Heartbreak is a necessary evil. It is only through experiencing some of the deepest, darkest, most difficult moments in our lives that we recognize when we arrive where we are supposed to be, that it was all worth it. It all makes sense.

Bless the broken road that leads us right to where we need to be. Life is full of ups and downs, twists and turns. Painful experiences and challenges come to us all, but it is through these opportunities that we get the chance to build character and see our growth develop. It takes courage to fight back from heartbreak. To have courage in our most vulnerable, darkest times when we feel so empty, is when we start to see in color again.

The universe always has our back no matter what. No matter how tough some of our days will be, it is important to feel the pain, acknowledge it, honour it, learn from it and keep moving forward. Keep. Moving. Forward. I promise what awaits us will be worth it.

The loss of that relationship was excruciatingly painful. Many days felt too unbearable to continue. He was my first love and my true soulmate. He got me. He understood every single part of my being. He was able to make me feel things in a way no one else possibly could. It felt as though we were one soul in two bodies. We had the most powerful force between us which felt so deep and so connected. A bond only we could feel and understand. He lit my heart and soul on fire. I unquestionably lost a piece of me when our circumstances forced us apart.

He will always be the brightest northern light in my life. And I will be forever grateful for the phenomenal memories we made together. I grew so much as a person because of him. He showed me a love that was extraordinary and undeniably powerful. He taught me many things. Most importantly, he taught me how incredibly beautiful love is and what is possible in this lifetime when you lead with love. He set the bar high, there is no doubt about it. In doing so, I learned what it meant to love and to be loved wholeheartedly. I understood what I needed, wanted and deserved in a life partner.

So to him, I say, thank you. Thank you for being such an incredible chapter in my life. Thank you for showing me what true love looks like. Thank you for being courageous enough to take a chance on me, on us, when we had a whole world between us. Thank you for every second we spent together and apart. You always made me feel safe, loved and beautiful. I don't have any regrets. We were exactly where we were supposed to be together in those moments in time. I will cherish every single second we shared until my last breath on this earth.

The beauty in the connections we make in this lifetime is, it is our perception, interpretation and acknowledgement that creates our reality. In the end, isn't that the magic of the human experience?

Don't forget to bless your broken road.

Epilogue

L   ittle did I know how much this relationship with Alex would shape me into the person I have become. Like a river shapes a stone, it would be the catalyst for my great love of love and my value for human connection.

The connection between couples is my deepest passion. So much so, that I have made it my life work. For years I have wanted to write this book. Timing though, is everything. When I finally decided in 2018, four years ago to start writing, I didn't get past the first few paragraphs. Not because I didn't have the time to write, but because the quality of what I was able to write at that time wouldn't suffice.

As time passed, the subtle nudges kept coming to me. Yet reflections of my past, and thoughts of how I would tell my story in a way that would do it justice still seemed overwhelming, to say the least.

In January of 2019, I took a leap of faith and opened my spa inside of a holistic wellness center. To say I was scared shitless would be an understatement. I would be among some incredible humans, next to which I didn't feel worthy enough. Who was I to be a part of a team that included a long list of medical practitioners and extraordinary women who were highly successful, intelligent, and the kind of people who selflessly changed the world for the better? People I had admired long before ever being a part of the team. I wasn't of this calibre. I didn't deserve to be included in this space.

This was nonsense. Complete bullshit. Of course, I was worthy. Glowing testimonial after glowing testimonial led to hundreds of amazing testimonials, and finally I accepted the fact that yes, maybe I was worthy. The team also empowered me and stopped at nothing to make sure I felt included.

After my experiences with Alex, I couldn't help but be enchanted by love. I consider myself to be a very sensual being, which transcends into the treatments I give at the spa. Inside my heart and soul, I have a deep connection to and understanding of sensual energy that I wanted to share with others.

One of the most common things clients would say to me in my practice is, "I wish you could teach my partner how to massage me like this." I realized there was a common thread - a common NEED presenting itself. Women and men were expressing their need to be touched, and in a way that they weren't experiencing enough or sometimes even at all with their partner. I understood deeply how important touch was to build a BEAUTIFUL sense of connection in loving relationships, so after hearing it again and again, I couldn't ignore this commonality between my clients. We've developed a world designed to create more connection than ever before, yet somehow, much of the digital age has severed connection or fostered inauthentic connection. I knew I wanted to do something to change this.

From that, I created a video — Ignite Together. It is a guided date night in experience for couples to do in the privacy of their home. My goal was for them to cultivate intimacy and connection, like the kind I felt when I was with him. In the video, couples practice eye gazing, deep breathing together, simple partner yoga poses and finally they learn massage techniques to use on one another that feel really great! If I could help one couple feel the magic I felt with him it would be more than worth it.

After the release of the video, I created an- experience where couples come to the spa to have me teach them in-person. I am able to provide many techniques that couples can take with them into their marriage for the rest of their lives.

Through my teachings, I get to witness transformational experiences for the couples who come into my space.

Working alongside such talented, knowledgeable, kind and loving people, I began to see my passions peek through. I started to think differently, and speak differently. I was seeing positive shifts and growth in myself that I never expected. Finally,

I felt ready to sit down and make this story come to life on paper.

As for Alex, we haven't had contact since that night he left me in Athens.

Will we ever see each other again? That remains to be seen. What I do know for certain is that he will forever occupy a spot in my heart. I will always care for him beyond measure. No matter what he does or where life takes him, I hope he carries a piece of me within him, too.

Acknowledgments

My darling husband Armand, to whom I owe my deepest gratitude. You are incredibly selfless, loving, understanding and compassionate. Thank you for keeping the fort together, enabling me to take the time I needed to write this book. It takes a special soul and a special love and understanding to be in your position. Without your love and support, this would not have been possible. You came into my path to show me a life I could not have dreamed of. Thank you. Because of you, I will forever bless my broken road. I love you, endlessly.

Nikolas and Lukas, my sweet boys. If I knew that the pain I would go through in my life would bring me to you, I would do it a million times over. My hope is that you know that no matter what happens in your life you will always be loved, guided and supported. Heartbreak and pain are a part of life. Feel it all fully and no matter what, please keep moving forward. There is so much beauty and so many incredible experiences for you to have in this lifetime. Don't deny yourself of any opportunities because of your fear of the process or your perceived thoughts on the intentions and limitations of others. The world, my loves is your oyster.

Remember to always be grateful and kind. I love you both with my entire heart and soul.

My dearest Sarah, I cannot in all the words of the world find the right ones to adequately let you know how much it means to me to have a piece of you etched into this book. I would never have been able to write this book before I met you. I tried. I could not have dreamed of a greater mentor and friend. From you, I have learned so much about myself and life. Thank you for your guidance and for always inspiring and believing in me. Because of you, I dream bigger. I am in awe of you and the way you so beautifully and authentically show up in this world each day. You are made of stardust and magic. I hope through reading this book you see glimpses of the teachings you've passed on to me. I am so damn grateful for you every single day. Thank you from the bottom of my heart for everything. You are truly an earth angel. I love you so much.

To my parents, thank you for allowing me to experience so many amazing trips to Greece throughout my life. This story would not have been possible without your generosity. Thank you for your trust, confidence and support in allowing me to find my own way. I love you.

Shannon, I am so thankful for your unconditional love and friendship. Thank you for reading this book more times than you probably care to remember. I appreciated your constant source of support and encouragement while I wrote this book. I love you, my friend.

Stathis, when I set out to find someone who was on that flight with me September 11, 2001, I had no idea I would find you - a crew member. Thank you so much for your kindness, for your quick replies and your willingness to help. Thank you for confirming the memories I had of being on that flight during one of the most horrific times in our history. Φιλάκια.

Over time, I have learned that vulnerability leads to growth and magic. Initially, it wasn't easy to share this book. To the beautiful souls who read my unpolished, raw version: Shannon A., Emma S., Jenny M., Kim H., Kati M., and Catherine N., thank you for empowering me with your generous thoughts and feedback. You were all instrumental in my journey to becoming an author.

Lastly, thank you Universe for always delivering ordinary and extraordinary miracles into my life. I am forever grateful.

Printed in Great Britain
by Amazon